LEARN TO JUDGE CHARACTER

LEARN TO JUDGE CHARACTER

A Guide to the Science and Art of Reading the
Character of the Men and Women you meet

BY
MAX CROMBIE

Fully Illustrated

W. FOULSHAM & CO., LTD.
LONDON • NEW YORK • TORONTO •
CAPE TOWN • SYDNEY

W. Foulsham & Company Limited
Yeovil Road, Slough, Berkshire, SL1 4JH

ISBN 0-572-01440-6

Copyright © 1987 W. Foulsham & Co. Ltd.

All rights reserved.
The Copyright Act (1956) prohibits (subject to certain very limited exceptions) the making of copies of any copyright work or of a substantial part of such a work, including the making of copies by photocopying or similar process. Written permission to make a copy or copies must therefore normally be obtained from the publisher in advance. It is advisable also to consult the publisher if in any doubt as to the legality of any copying which is to be undertaken.

Printed in Great Britain
by Hollen Street Press, Slough, Berkshire

CONTENTS

1 GENERAL INTRODUCTION 6
2 THE THREE RULING TYPES 11
3 THE HEAD AND THE HAIR 24
4 THE EYES AND EYEBROWS 39
5 THE NOSE AND EARS 48
6 THE MOUTH, LIPS AND CHIN 57
7 THE HANDS AND GESTURES 66
8 POSTURE AND WALK 79
9 THE CHOICE OF A PROFESSION OR PURSUIT 87
INDEX 94

CHAPTER 1

GENERAL INTRODUCTION

BEYOND question, character reading is a most fascinating pursuit. The ability to judge character—to learn of the inward man by reading the outward signs—is at once a source of pleasure and profit. It would be going too far, perhaps, to say that a knowledge of how character evidences itself in visible signs is necessary to self-protection in these days of highly competitive living; but it is certainly true that the ability to discover with what manner of person one is dealing is a most valuable asset.

Forewarned is forearmed, and the person who is a shrewd and practised judge of character is far less likely to be hoodwinked or imposed upon, than the one who is forced simply to take people for granted, through sheer inability to 'read the signs'. We speak of 'seeing through' persons—but they are usually the transparent ones, or maybe we only 'see through' them after long acquaintance. The character reader 'sees through' everyone. He does not find out the rogue by becoming his victim. He recognises the coquette, and refuses to take her seriously. He knows the fine, straightforward types and trusts them. When the characters of the people you meet are an open book to you, you get a lot more fun and interest out of life. You can never be bored. You are studying the most intensely interesting thing in the world—human nature. We are all character readers, more or less, but the trouble with most of us is that we do not consciously train and develop our powers of judging character. We recognise the extreme types—the Uriah Heeps and the Cheerybles—but we are beaten by the great variety of what may be termed 'middle types'. It is the object of this volume to introduce you to this fascinating study of human nature, called character reading.

Character reading, or physiognomy, to give it the correct name, is one of the oldest of the sciences. We have records of its practice nearly 2,400 years ago, and it was unquestionably known for thousands of years before that. Through the ages has been stored up a vast accumulation of data on the subject.

Character judgement is not a trivial game, but is based on a large number of well-established scientific principles.

Certainly we have all about us abundant evidence of the close connection between character and outward appearance. However much we attempt outwardly to dissimilate, we are our own true selves in our thoughts, and those thoughts write unmistakable messages in our faces, reflect themselves in our eyes, stamp themselves upon our features and influence our bodily poise, gestures and walk.

How plainly the emotions write themselves on the features! The bereaved mother or widow—her sorrow is poignantly expressed in her features, in her bodily poise, in her gestures. Great joy as well as great sorrow tells its story in the features. Those whose lives have been difficult or sorrowful carry the signs. On the other hand, those who have passed through life on an easy, pleasant path exhibit the tranquillity which has been the keynote of their existence.

It might be said with truth: 'By their habits ye shall know them,' for habits have their distinguishing signs. We cannot easily mistake the man or woman who habitually practises excess in any shape or form. Indulgence in the grosser material pleasures writes its story in the features. At the other extreme, the person habitually studious carries the signs of his or her application to things mental.

Having very briefly indicated the value of character reading and shown its intimate connection with everyday things, this introductory chapter may be concluded with a few words of important warning.

The broad plan upon which this book has been written is first to examine the three ruling types of mankind and then to examine the separate parts from which we read character, beginning with the shape of the head and then working down from the hair, through the features, to the hands, then to the posture, walk and so on.

It must not, however, be thought that a person's character can be read from any single feature, or even pair of features.

You may know someone with fine red hair and a pronounced Roman nose. From these two features you might deduce that the person was of a somewhat passionate and sensitive disposition, but possessed of considerable power to sway others. It would, however, be quite wrong to give this as a complete reading of that person's character.

Character judgement, to be worthy of having any reliance placed upon it, should be the result of a careful consideration of *all* the data which can be gleaned from all sources—not merely the hair and nose but the shape of the head, the kind of brow, the eyes, eyebrows, ears, mouth, chin, hands, physique, walk, voice, etc. Never attempt to read character from a partial analysis. Every feature either enhances or modifies every other.

If you are hoping that this book will teach you how to read a man's character from a rapid glance at his profile, you will be disappointed. When a man tells you that he can read character at a glance, know him for a trifler with the truth—and begin to read his character as it should be read, from *all* the signs he exhibits.

It is always a sound plan to proceed from the known to the unknown—especially when tackling a new subject. It will be very necessary for you to check off your readings against what you know of the person. If you read the character of a stranger, you may, probably will, be quite unable to know if and to what extent you have scored correctly. Very much better is it to let your first attempts at character reading be confined to those you know really well.

As you know no one better than yourself, you should begin by analysing your own character, from what you can see in the mirror and from photographs which show you in profile. As you proceed chapter by chapter through this book, apply the principles to your own self.

Your next attempts at character reading should be on near relatives (you need not disclose what you discover!) with whom you come in daily contact. Here you can and should check off what you deduce against what you know. You may, for example, discover a sign which (alone) means hasty temper. If you know the person to be even-tempered, look for other signs indicative of traits which counteract the hastiness of temper, or keep it in check. You will assuredly find them, for they are there.

You can next practise on your friends, then on casual acquaintances and lastly on total strangers. A final word of warning—GO SLOWLY.

I have used the pronoun 'he' throughout the book, but, except where indicated, the comments can refer to either sex.

CHAPTER 2

THE THREE RULING TYPES

From the earliest times, philosophers have attempted to place human beings into certain categories, to classify them as *types*. The names given to these types have varied with the progress of thought, but the nature of the classifications has remained singularly unchanged. It is the most convincing evidence in support of the scientific soundness of physiognomy that, after over two thousand years and with all our immense collateral learning to help us, we are adhering to very much the same categories as the ancients.

To come directly to our point, human beings fall into three main groups, which are termed Motive, Vital and Mental respectively. Each of these three main types may be recognised by a characteristic shape of the full face. The diagrams in the text illustrate the three pure types.

Now before you attempt to classify yourself as a Motive, Vital or Mental type, let me state very clearly that pure types are *extremely rare*—in fact, some authorities maintain that the 100 per cent pure types do not exist.

It is certainly true that the overwhelming majority of people are, as is only to be expected after all, hybrids or 'mixtures' in this matter of type. But if we learn the characteristics of the pure types, practice will soon give us the ability to read the hybrids. In certain cases, the types are so mixed that a sort of 'neutral' character is evolved, one characteristic cancelling out another.

It will be best, first, to examine the pure types, and then to consider the hybrids.

THE MOTIVE TYPE

All the time you are considering this type, keep the geometrical figure of the square prominently in mind, for it is the keynote of the Motive character.

The Motive type is built on the square, and acts on the square. The man of the Motive type can be recognised by his squareness of feature.

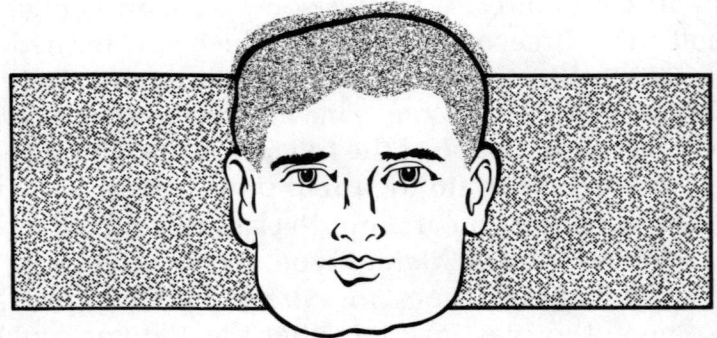

Fig. 1   The Motive—or square—type

He is by no means unintelligent, because he has breadth of forehead—a sign of mental ability of an essentially practical nature. While not a 'low-brow', he is not of a studious nature usually, nor is he a dreamer or idealist.

The Motive type is a good planner and organiser, but only as far as it concerns getting things done. If you have ever known a person who is always anxious to 'stop talking and get on with it', that person is either of the pure Motive type or, what is far more likely, a hybrid with a strong bias towards the Motive temperament in his make-up.

The squareness of feature which is so characteristic of the Motive type is continued in the frame, which is square built with large bones. A square head on square shoulders, a square frame standing four-square to the world—there you have the Motive type. Built for action, not admiration, the Motive type is not graceful, not curved, but angular. Ever a doer and not a dreamer, this type possesses abundant energy and is not afraid to use it.

Amazing capacity for work marks the Motive type, and this is often the explanation of the material success which the type achieves. He succeeds less by brilliance than by sheer solid worth and doggedness.

So much for the physical characteristics, by means of which we may recognise the Motive type. Now for mental characteristics to confirm our first judgement.

Keep the geometrical figure of the square—or, better still, the cube—in mind, for 'squareness' remains the keynote. The man of the predominantly Motive type is always strictly businesslike; he has 'no use' for the subtleties of life. Flattery leaves him cold; he is not to be cajoled and certainly not to be driven. It is impossible to persuade him to act against his better judgement. He is usually inclined to be self-opinionated, but can be convinced by sound, solid reasoning.

The Motive type makes a capable businessman and is best seen in an executive position, with others under him to attend to details. He is not swayed unduly by his emotions, and his solidity is accompanied by stolidity. He is not easily moved—as a cube is not easily moved. He does not sway this way or that, but stands firm to the winds of popular opinion and adversity.

The Motive type has, as a rule, considerable powers of observation—certainly so, when the eyebrows are full and overhang the eyes closely. Not much escapes him. He has also marked constructive ability, but it is of a practical nature. He is a builder, but of material and concrete things—not a weaver of gossamer dreams and Utopian schemes. Firmness and self-reliance would be expected of the cube, and they are characteristic of the Motive type. Slow in anger, he is formidable when aroused.

The squareness of the Motive type is carried into his dealings. He likes everything to be 'fair and square' and above board. He makes a fetish of correctness of conduct and is intolerant of hole-in-the-corner methods. He is prepared to carry out his part of a contract, even if it breaks him to do it, and expects to be treated in the same way. 'Soft-soap' methods anger him, and he is quick to resent anything resembling undue familiarity.

Summarised, the outstanding characteristic of the Motive type is solid, sterling worth and integrity.

THE VITAL TYPE

The Vital type is in many ways the antithesis of the Motive type, but this does not mean that the two types cannot blend in one individual, for they frequently do so.

Exactly as the Motive type can be represented by the geometrical figures of the square and the cube, so the Vital type can be visualised by means of the circle and the sphere. Roundness is the keynote here.

The man of the Vital type has a full-moon face, but in most cases the circle has become lengthened, as it were, and the oval is obtained. The oval-faced man is predominantly Vital.

Rotundity of figure is characteristic, too. The Vital person exhibits a tendency to plumpness, which is quite in keeping with his love of creature comforts. In the Vital type, the neck is usually short and full.

The Vital type takes its name from the fact that, in the members of this group, we find the vital organs well developed. Persons of the Vital type are more intensely alive than either the Motive or Mental types. They are full of vitality, energy and driving force. Often they possess that subtle something called (for want of a better term) personal magnetism—that peculiar vital force which attracts others.

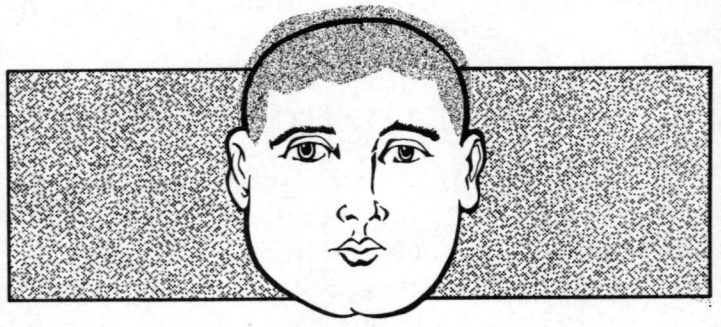

Fig. 2   The Vital—or round—type

Their vitality is evidenced in brightness of eye, high colour and a cheerful countenance. You never meet a pure Vital person who is of a despondent nature—their very vitality gives them hope and is incompatible with despondency.

Though the Vital person is built in a series of curves, there is nothing ungainly about him. Small hands and feet are characteristic of this type—it is as though they taper at the base like a top. It is well known that round-faced stoutish men are usually excellent dancers, when they can overcome that natural disinclination to exert themselves, and can be persuaded to dance. That is because they are light on their feet—poised on their tapered end. Again, their vitality gives them buoyancy. Exactly the same applies to women.

Those of the Vital type are energetic—how can they be otherwise, with their store of vitality? But nonetheless they are very partial to the good things of life—fond of ease and creature comforts. While not mere gourmands, they appreciate the need of stoking their vital fires.

Their superabundance of vitality makes them impulsive—they are apt to dash off without paying great regard to direction. They succeed well in business because of their inexhaustible energy, and because they can be, and are, so contagiously enthusiastic about things which capture their fancy. The Vital type of person makes an excellent salesman, commercial traveller or auctioneer.

Predominantly Vital persons are also excellent company and make good entertainers. They have the knack of imparting some of their enthusiasm to their audience. Invariably cheerful themselves, they prefer lively company and dislike morose individuals intensely. Often sporting, they are lovers of the open air—they drink it in as one of the most necessary sources of their vitality. They are sometimes changeable and fickle—remember how easily a sphere is rolled this way or that. They can usually be moved by an appeal to their love of physical well-being.

In business, persons of the Vital type are not likely to be moved by an appeal to pure reason or by coldly logical arguments. They are more susceptible to an appeal to the emotions—to the heart as opposed to the head. In this they differ radically from the pure Motive type. Generally speaking, they are not slow to take action when the appeal has been appropriately made.

Summarised, the dominant characteristic of the Vital type is smoothly flowing vitality.

THE MENTAL TYPE

In some ways, this is the highest type of all, as the name suggests. At the same time, the pure (or nearly so) Mental type is often rather an insufferable sort of person; his very superior brain power makes him so. He is apt to be contemptuous of and impatient with those who fail to 'jump to it' as rapidly, mentally, as he does.

A brief digression may be made here to point out that a pure type is today so rare as to be abnormal. Through thousands of years we have become so mixed in type that a pure type is really an atavism or 'throw-back'. The pure type is abnormal, and all extremes and abnormalities are undesirable and bad from the character point of view.

The pure Mental type has a face roughly kite-shaped. The exact shape of the upper part of the head determines in which direction his mental superiority will evidence itself, but of that we shall have something to say later.

The most marked characteristic of the Mental type is the high development of that part of the head situated above the eyebrows. The lower part of the face tends to come to a point at the chin. The head of the Mental type person is large relative to his body, and his whole physical make-up seems subordinated to his highly developed brain. Quite often he runs to weediness of frame.

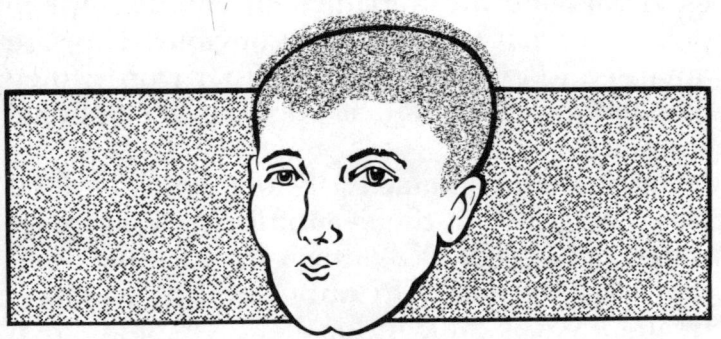

Fig. 3   The Mental—or kite-shape—type

Persons of this type have delicate features, finely chiselled, with bright and expressive eyes. Being slight of build, they are not ungraceful, though extreme examples of the Mental type often completely disregard their personal appearance. This type is not infrequently a 'ladies' man', feeling an irresistible attraction to the opposite sex. This may be accounted for by the fact that their superior brain power, and rather contemptuous treatment of the Vital and Motive members of their own sex, is not condusive to their popularity among men. Again, their devotion to things mental for the greater part of their time enforces a periodical reaction towards things physical.

The mental characteristics of this type are exactly what we would expect them to be. They are exceedingly rapid, but also clear and deep thinkers. Because of their highly developed brains, persons of this type are quick to grasp essentials and are impatient of any attempt to point out what they regard as obvious. They are appealed to by cold logic—in other words, they respond to intellectual, as opposed to emotional stimulus.

Refinement is characteristic of them; also good taste and a love of the beautiful. For the grosser things of life they have little use, and quite often they carry idealism to impracticable lengths—frequently it is difficult for them to 'come down to earth'. Possessed of lively imaginations, they are the thinkers of the race—the mental and intellectual pioneers.

This type can be possessed of rare moral courage, but they are not exactly lion-hearted physically. They possess such vivid imaginative powers that they suffer pain before it comes. But when faced with fear-inspiring things, they often act with rare courage, because their mentality induces a very clear conception of what is their duty and insists upon its performance.

Persons of the Mental type are continually

probing and asking 'Why?' They are impatient of 'I don't know'. They want chapter and verse quoted in support of any claims made, and will detect the weakness in any argument with disconcerting directness and suddenness. They are quick to lose interest and confidence where the information they demand is not forthcoming.

Summarised, the characteristics of the pure Mental type are exceptional brain power and contemptuous intolerance or pitying patronage of those less well-endowed mentally. The Mental type is much easier to get on with when modified by a strong dash of the Vital or Motive.

THE HYBRIDS

In view of the detailed attention given to each of the three main types, it will not be necessary to deal at length with the combination or hybrid types. Of the three ruling types, the Vital may be taken as the most important, because it is the most generally useful type, coming mid-way between the stolidity of the Motive type and the brilliant instability of the Mental. For this reason, the combination types in which the Vital is represented are the best.

It usually happens that there is a bias in favour of one or other of the parts—that is, we seldom have a combination, for example, of the Motive and the Vital in which the two types are evenly balanced. The type which is dominant is written first, and the four combinations of the Motive with the Vital, and the Vital with the Mental are expressed as follows:

    Motive-Vital   Vital-Mental
    Vital-Motive   Mental-Vital

It will be observed that I have not dealt with the possibility of a combination of the Motive and the Mental types—the two extremes, if we regard the Vital as the middle type.

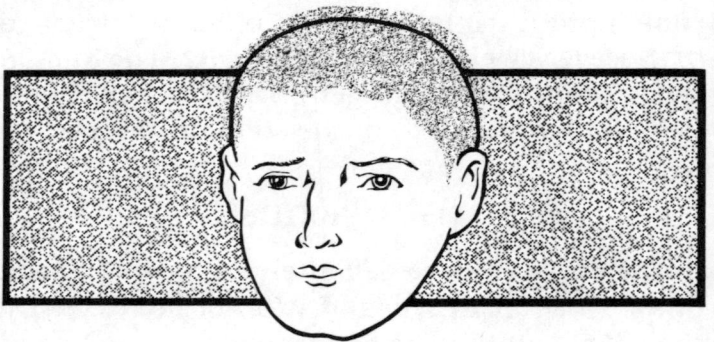

Fig. 4   The Vital-Mental type

While not going so far as to say that such a combination is impossible, it is not very likely. The characteristics can be blended, but almost always with the Motive-Mental combination we have a strong dash of the Vital. In fact, as stated above, some authorities state that pure types are never found, combinations of pairs of types but rarely, and that the overwhelming majority of us are blends of all three types—either with one type very strong and the other two weak, or with one type very weak and the other two strong in equal measure.

When it is realised what an infinite variety of combinations we can get by blending the three types in different degrees of strength, it will be realised that if we attempt to read character by paying attention only to the Motive, Vital and Mental characteristics, we are going to experience great difficulty in 'placing' some persons.

This is where all else that goes to make up character reading comes in. The judgement of character by means of a knowledge of the types is an attempt to judge from the *whole*. As character reading is an analytical process, it follows that we can get upon much firmer ground by examining separate features—by having regard to the *parts* as opposed to the whole. This is dealt with in the remainder of this book.

But we must not imagine that a knowledge of the three ruling types is of little or no use to us. It is of very real value—especially when circumstances make a detailed analysis of the other person impossible. For example, a salesman should pay the closest attention to the three ruling types, for the reason that he cannot very well ask a prospective buyer to 'sit quite still' for half an hour while he makes an analytical reading of his character. The classification of a person as Mental-Vital, Vital-Motive, Motive-Vital-Mental, or whatever the combination may be, is an excellent starting point. We can then proceed to read the character analytically from the parts, and so obtain confirmation of our first provisional judgement upon the whole.

CHAPTER 3

THE HEAD AND THE HAIR

WHEN dealing with the three ruling types, we had a great deal to say about the shape of the head, but many details remain to be treated.

Beginning at the top, the rounded or dome-shaped head is indicative of a leaning towards things spiritual. Marked top cranial development is a sign of high moral character. Such attributes as benevolence and veneration will be strongly in evidence. Persons of deeply religious temperament have high, dome-shaped heads. Where the head comes to a point at the top, firmness which may amount to obstinacy is indicated.

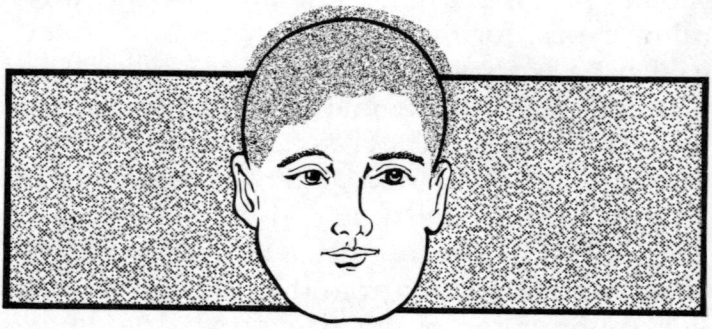

Fig. 5   The moral head

The head which is large and full at the back, level with the forehead, marks the person of a more wordly turn of mind, but one of warm affections. The head that is flat at the back is indicative of a love of 'number one'—conceit, egotism and selfishness.

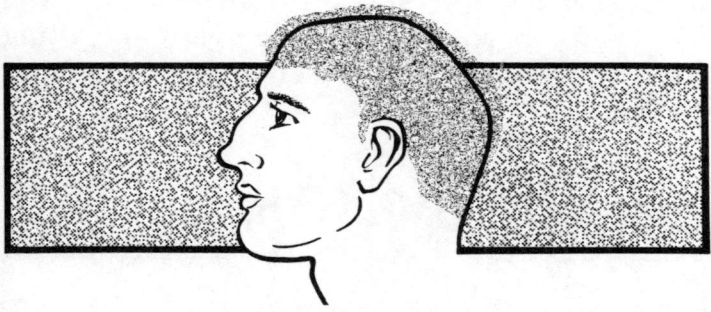

Fig. 6   The material head

It is a mistake to imagine that a low brow or forehead is the sign of stupidity or absence of mental ability. Narrowness, not lowness, is the sign of poor mentality. Do not credit the person with a narrow head, from temple to temple, with the possession of much brain.

Marked development just above the ears only, where such development is not continued to the top of the head, is a bad sign, being symptomatic of the qualities of deceptiveness. Do not trust a person with 'bumps' over the ears.

Development in a more forward direction, over the temples and not over the ears, is indicative of idealism and imagination. Social reformers—whose ideas of how to achieve the millenium are more beautiful than practicable—have this development.

From foreheads we can learn a great deal, as is to be expected. There are three main types of forehead—the *bulging*, the *straight* and the *receding*. Generally speaking, forehead development is indicative of reasoning powers, but the bulging forehead, in conjunction with the jutting chin, is a sign of an obstinate and stubborn nature.

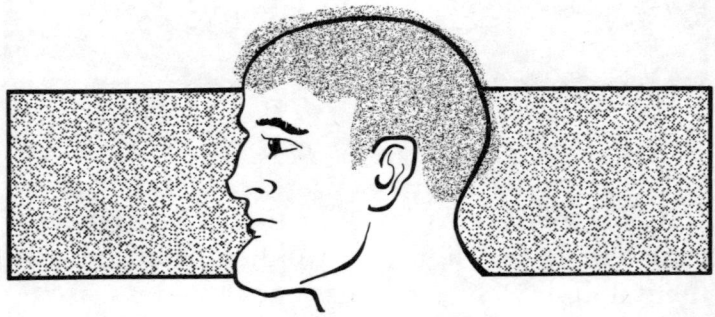

Fig. 7   The stubborn head

Experts in physiognomy are generally agreed that the straight, upright forehead is the best and the sharply receding forehead the worst, in what they indicate. The best type of mentality is displayed in a forehead which not only is straight but also wide and fairly high. Look out for this type of forehead among your clever friends. Unquestionably, the high wide forehead is the sign of an intelligence and mental development above the average.

The low wide (note how the wideness is always important) forehead is good, belonging generally to the person of an imaginative and romantic turn of mind. Many writers of fictional romances have this type of forehead. In fact, the low, broad forehead is characteristic of the creative-imaginative worker, the journalist and novelist, the author and playwright. They write more from intuition than from knowledge gained by diligent study. They are essentially persons who give out—that is, they impart knowledge and information to others, or give out the figments of their brains in the form of fiction.

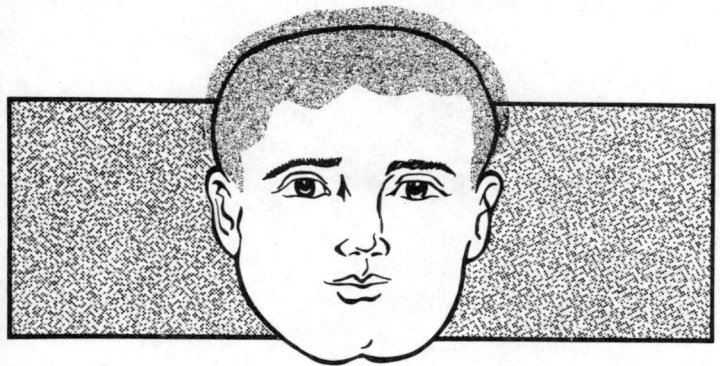

Fig. 8   The imaginative head

The high, narrow (by comparison) forehead indicates the person of studious habits. Such people painstakingly acquire a vast store of knowledge, but do not, as a rule, reimpart any of it. They are takers-in, not givers-out.

The bulging forehead is the sign of the slow and heavy, as opposed to the nimble, thinker. This forehead, generally speaking, belongs to the plodder and not to the brilliant class of worker. The more pronounced the bulge, the greater the degree of stolidity, merging into stubborness. The square forehead is a characteristic of the Motive type, and a particularly ponderous, heavy mentality is found behind the squarish, bulging forehead.

The sharply receding type of forehead—the one that shoots straight back from immediately above the eyebrows—is indicative of a very low order of mentality; craft and cunning should be looked for in connection with it.

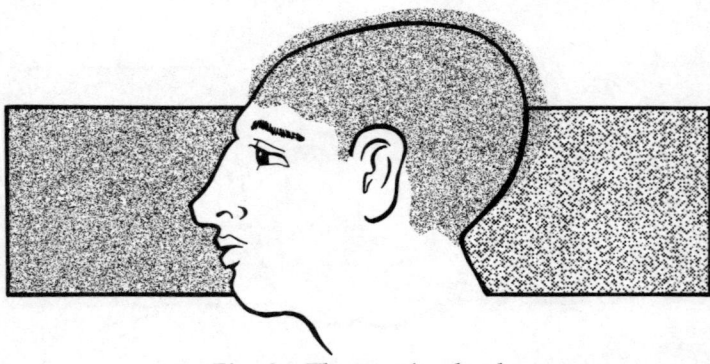

Fig. 9   The cunning head

Good development of the forehead above the eyes betokens power of observation, which will be strong in proportion to the amount of the localised bulge. Men of the predominantly Motive type usually have this development, as do successful detectives. Development between the eyebrows is generally accepted as a sign of a retentive memory.

The perceptive faculties, then, are indicated by development immediately above the eyebrows. We must be careful not to credit the person with good development in this region with a receding forehead. The forehead is usually of the upright type, but the strong development above the eyes gives an appearance of receding.

Above the perceptive faculties we have the reflective region, which lies along the forehead on the level of the hat brim. Put on a trilby-style hat and draw your finger across your forehead as close under the brim as you can, and you will be touching the reflective region. The deep thinkers are well developed here. Our great scientists are strong in the reflective region.

Good development in that part of the forehead which lies high up above the outer ends of the

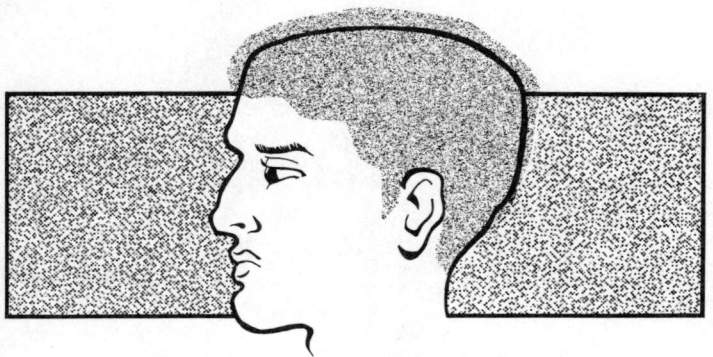

Fig. 10   The intellectual head

eyes is a dependable sign of considerable intellect.

Good development of the lower back part of the head is a sign of a material mind—a love of home and children, eating and drinking and the good things of life, the opposite sex, and so on. Underdevelopment in this region is not good, because it indicates a want of vitality. Of such a person we might say that he or she seems 'only half alive'.

The ambitious type of head is that which goes 'upwards and onwards'—that is, after the forehead has been passed, the head continues to slope up, to reach its highest point above the line of the back of the neck. Conversely, the head which is highest in the front and slopes down to the back is that of the person wanting in self-esteem—the self-effacing, benevolent type, always prone to be exploited and 'put upon'.

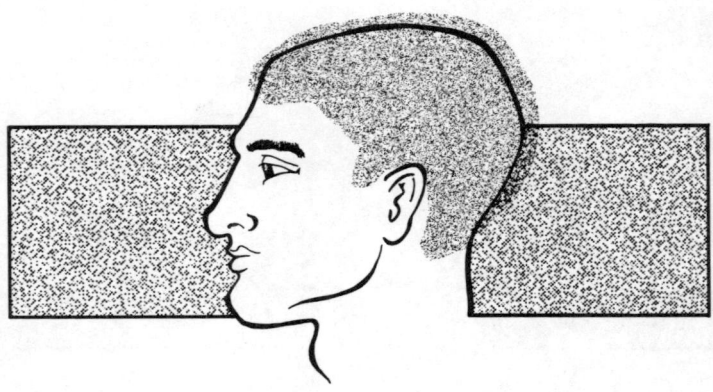

Fig. 11   The ambitious head

So much for the head. Now a few words about what it rests upon, the neck. What we learn from the neck depends upon its length and thickness. At the two extremes, we have the long thin neck and the short thick neck. The first is indicative of shyness, timidity and diffidence; the second of strength, courage and endurance. Aggressiveness to the point of pugnacity is indicated by the short thick neck. We speak of persons going at things 'like a bull at a gate', and of being 'bull-necked'. They are the type without finesse, who use their heads, not to think with, but as battering rams.

It will, therefore, be gathered that the happy mean is reached in the fairly short, fairly thick neck of the person possessed of strength without brutality, courage without a foolish contempt for danger and endurance without pigheadedness.

We must, however, differentiate in this matter between men and women. It is more natural for a woman to have a long neck than a man. Therefore, what would be a long neck on a man would be normal on a woman. Conversely, what would be a short, thick neck when found in a woman would be quite normal on a man.

Poets usually have quite a lot to say about the tresses of the ladies who happen to be occupying their thoughts at the moment, and it is true that we can learn quite a lot about a person's character from the hair. For those who have become ensnared by the beauty of a young woman's hair, we must hasten to utter a word of caution against the straight-haired blonde, and another of commendation for the wavy-haired brunette. The first, alas, is the coquette and the second the constant lover—usually.

The quality and colour of the hair must be considered carefully by the serious student of physiognomy. From the colour of the hair we learn of what is called the pigmentation of the body, of the presence or absence of certain elements in the physical make-up. Any attempt to judge character from the hair alone is almost certain to fail, because we cannot go far enough. What it reveals must be confirmed or modified by knowledge gained from other sources.

To begin with a general observation, hair and energy go together. The thicker and more luxuriant the hair, the greater the strength or energy. Naturally hairless, or almost hairless, persons are usually not strong. The hairy people normally live outdoor lives, for which their hairy protection from the elements suits them. The non-hairy persons lead sheltered lives. Consider these points in connection with man's tendency to become less hairy as he becomes more civilized. The hairy persons are the pioneers, the explorers and dwellers in the wilderness. The non-hairy persons are the thinkers, the planners, the schemers.

Once more, consider sex. Luxuriant hair on the head is more natural in a woman than in a man, but a general hairiness is most abnormal in a woman. For this reason, hair poverty in a woman is a much surer sign of poor vitality than it would be in a man. Conversely, general hairiness in a woman may be accepted as one sign of masculinity and the possession of traits of character more usually found in men.

Let us begin by examining the things to be learnt from the quality of the hair. Hair can be short and crisp or long and dank-looking. The first is better; a tendency to wave is a good sign also.

Hard, coarse, wiry hair, while indicative of qualities of virility and endurance, is also the sign of a certain hardness of nature, especially in a woman. In brief, 'hard' haired persons are prone to be hard-hearted. On the other hand, those with soft, silky hair are sympathetic and gentle by nature. The silky-haired person will never wittingly hurt anyone's feelings if he or she can possibly help it. If a silky-haired man has to act in a manner which gives pain, he feels much of that pain himself. The same applies, of course, and in a greater degree, to women.

The wiry kind of hair, especially when it is mid or dark brown, is usually found on the self-reliant person. Sometimes that self-reliance amounts to self-sufficiency; but generally speaking, the wiry-haired individual is a fine type of worker, possessed of energy and initiative.

Soft hair, however, is indicative of a gentleness of demeanour, a love of Nature, a desire for peace. The soft-haired person is imaginative and emotional, easily moved by an appeal to their 'soft side', which is dominant. Curling hair is a sign of a warm, affectionate disposition. When the hair is soft, that affection will be gentle—respectful admiration as a rule; but when it is wiry, the affection may show itself in a more active, not to say domineering, manner. The more red in the colour, the more the passion exhibited.

Hair that grows quickly goes with a generous nature; hair that hardly seems to grow at all indicates irritability, amounting to rank bad temper. This fact has a physical explanation, and it is quite possible that with improved health the hair will begin to grow at its normal rate once more, when the bad temper will disappear.

Now to consider colour. The fairer the hair, generally, the greater the lack of perseverence, energy, driving force and the qualities which make for success in the face of adversity. Call to mind all the men you know who have achieved worthwhile success in face of repeated setbacks, and you will find them all dark-haired. Deepness of colour, especially when accompanied by a tendency to wave, may be accepted as a sign of strength of character.

The 'key' characteristics of the four groups of hair colour are: blonde, fickleness; brown, constancy; red or auburn, passion; black, sadness.

It is important for us to remember, however, that there is such a thing as a racial colour—of hair, eyes, complexion and so on. The Norsemen were racially very fair, the Jews were and are racially very dark haired. In these circumstances, we must ask ourselves to what extent the colouring is due to racial predisposition and make allowances accordingly.

Very fair hair, where it is not racial, is characteristic in persons of a dreamy, impracticable, listless nature. They are imaginative enough, but their imaginings seldom if ever lead to anything definite. They tend to drift through life, vaguely dissatisfied with their lot, complaining of their treatment, but lacking the driving force to be up and doing to alter things. Very fair hair indicates changeability in a marked degree. The ultra-blonde is often in and out of love half-a-dozen times before she settles down, if she ever does.

The next shade, real golden hair (not the pale straw-coloured shade dealt with above) also indicates a somewhat fickle temperament. The golden-haired person is fond of pleasure and wishes all the time to be entertained. Generally well disposed, such persons are prone to cause unhappiness by their fondness for pleasure and their fickleness. These negative qualities become less pronounced as the gold shade deepens towards that nondescript colour sometimes called 'mousy'.

A red gleam in the hair is no bad sign. Unmistakably red hair usually goes with keen intelligence and perceptiveness; but if the intelligence is misdirected (whether or not, depends on other traits in the character), the red-headed person will accomplish nothing very commendable or noteworthy in life.

Red hair, allied with certain other characteristics, is indicative of a tendency to employ physical force which may amount to brutality. This would certainly be so in persons of poor top cranial development, but with marked development behind the ear, level with and some small distance from it. Red pigment in the hair is in proportion to the animal part of us, but if the other qualities are well developed, this animal predominance will be kept in check.

Fine, soft, red hair, or hair with a strong tinge of red in it, is the sign of a person of lively habits and a dashing sort of temperament—especially if the individual is of the Vital type. Redness of hair also indicates self-assertiveness. Red-headed persons like to have their own way; they domineer. Not infrequently they are conceited, imagining they are quite wonderful. They are prone to be patronising in manner and are most surprised if they do not call forth admiration.

The person with red-brown hair is nature's fighter. Where combativeness is indicated by good development behind the ear and a couple of centimetres from it, and the region immediately behind the ear is poorly developed, courage to the point of recklessness will usually be found.

The person with red-brown hair, unless other restraining traits are well developed, will have much of the domineering tendency and self-assertiveness of the true red type. Persons of a brusque, boastful nature usually have red-brown hair of coarse texture.

In a more balanced temperament, reddish-brown hair indicates considerable strength of will. This strength of will is present in the reddish-brown type discussed in the preceding paragraph, but there it was ill-directed and showed itself in a bullying nature. The energy of the reddish-brown haired type leads to marked success in life, if it is controlled and directed in the proper manner. Tenacity of purpose, combined with this energy, is a practically irresistible combination.

People with frankly brown hair are easy to get along with, being well-disposed towards everyone. They are warm-hearted, naturally courteous, somewhat sensitive, responsive, hospitable, fond of home and children, anxious to think well of everyone and to be thought well of by them, and so on. Youthfulness of spirits is usually placed to their credit, with sound reason.

Brown-haired people are often sentimental, lovers of romance. They are the reverse of close-fisted, being generous to a fault. They make good travellers, being fond of roaming, but their love of home brings them back from their wanderings after a time.

Those with light-coloured hair are self-centred, and therefore unsympathetic, unless, as explained above, there is a racial predisposition towards blonde colouring. The more pigment there is in the hair, the more sympathy there is in the temperament. The dark-haired person shares your sorrow, when it leaves the fair one unmoved. Dark hair is usually found with a strong and ardent nature. Dark-haired persons are energetic, especially if the hair is short, crisp and inclined to wave or curl. Persons with long, straight dark hair are often energetic mentally, but lazy physically. The reason why dark hair is usually indicative of strength and energy is because it reveals the presence of iron in the system.

As we approach black hair, the characteristics ascribed to dark brown hair become more and more marked. Very few persons indeed have really black hair—so black that it looks bluish. Most persons who flatter themselves that they have black hair really have very dark brown. Look at such hair after it has been washed quite free of oily dressings, against the light, and the brownness is unmistakable.

Jet black hair is the accompaniment of a passionate nature, capable of strong feelings of jealousy. Indolence is more likely to be found than energy. When the hair is long and straight, the skin sallow and the cheek bones high, you have a person of a melancholy disposition. Fanaticism may also be present. Wild social reformers, prophets of blood-spilling and anarchy, are usually of the straight black-haired type. On the other hand, beware of assuming that all black-haired people are fanatics, since racial characteristics give no indication of individual character.

CHAPTER 4

THE EYES AND EYEBROWS

THE shrewd and experienced reader of character will pay the closest attention to the eyes, and we wish to draw attention to the manner in which the emotions shine out through the eyes, and how easy it is with a little practice to read the 'language of the eyes'.

As stated in the opening chapter, we are all of us in some degree readers of character, and we instinctively look to the eyes of the person we meet for the first time for some clue to character. If we see small, dark, narrowly set, piercing, crafty eyes, we are on our guard at once. If we see frank, open eyes of 'honest grey', well set and steady in gaze, we register a mental 'all's well'.

In examining the eyes for clues to character, we must pay attention to three main things: position, size and colour. These three points are not in order of importance.

Eyes set wide apart are indicative of an open and candid nature, while eyes set close together are a sign—a sure sign, usually—of secretiveness. Eyes that are the normal width apart signify normality of character—the normal distance apart being the width of one eye. Eyes which are exceptionally wide apart are usually found in the vacant type of face and are indicative of foolishness amounting in some cases to idiocy. Once more we would stress the point that, in character reading, all extremes should be regarded as bad signs. Eyes set very close together tell a tale of cunning, craftiness and deceit. They are found in persons with 'foxy' faces.

The size of the eye is important, but—as always—the information we get from this source must be checked off against that from all other sources. For example, eyes that are exceptionally large and open signify a fondness for society, especially of the opposite sex. In association with golden hair and lower back cranial development, this would point to a somewhat frivolous, pleasure-loving nature. But we frequently find large, open eyes associated with considerable forehead (intellectual) development. In this case we should expect to find the fondness for society modified into pleasure in associating with other persons of equal intellectual development, such as in attendance at gatherings which the frivolous pleasure-seeker would condemn as 'highbrow' and boring in the extreme.

The bulging eye is indicative of studiousness when it is not too pronounced, and when it is accompanied by high and somewhat narrow cranial development. The excessively bulging eye is a sign of stupidity. It will be noticed once more that abnormal development in any direction is not a good sign.

The clear, full eye signifies devotion to any pursuits in hand. The clear eye is indicative of good health and right habits of living, just as the dull bleary eye tells us the opposite story. Here, however, we must be sure that the dull eye is normal in the person under examination, and not merely the temporary result of ill health or mental overstrain.

Much can be learned from the gaze. It is an old, familiar challenge to 'look me in the eye and tell me . . .' whatever it is that difficulty is experienced in believing. The person of really deceitful nature can often bluff his way through this ordeal and does actually act the part of honesty of purpose. But the naturally straightforward person, tempted for once to practise deceit, succumbs and cannot meet the gaze of the challenger.

It is, however, a popular mistake to imagine that honesty of character is indicated by the person continuing to look the other 'straight in the eye'. It is the steadiness of the gaze which is important, not the direction. A long-sighted person finds it physically distressing to look a nearby person in the face for long. So some convenient object at a distance is selected and the gaze is fixed on that.

It is the shifty gaze which does not rest on any one thing for more than a moment or two which betrays the crafty, cunning nature. The dreamy, wistful gaze betokens a simple, trusting nature.

Heavy lids—hack writers love to call them 'langourous'—are associated with slow and sensuous natures. The sinuous foreign 'vamp' of the films has black eyes with heavy lids.

Lids which are partially dropped, so that half or nearly half of the pupil is covered, signify a penetrating, observant nature. Mark your own tendency partially to close your eyes when focusing something at a distance. There is a physical reason for this, but it is none-the-less sound from a character reading point of view.

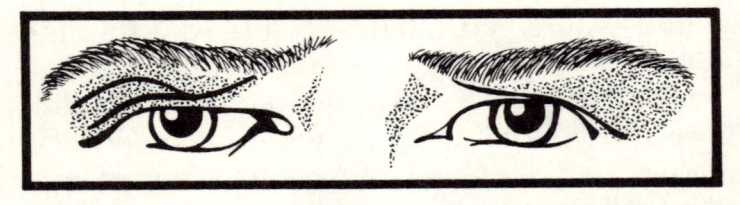

Fig. 12   Eyes and brows characteristic of an observant nature

Long lashes are a sign of vitality and of shrewd powers of observation. Absence of lashes is usually a sign of weak vision, poor powers of observation and lack of vitality and talent generally.

Eyes to which tears come readily—for example, when the person laughs or is moved in any way—signify a sympathetic nature, when found in a person of fine character. When found in persons of a deceitful nature, the tears are of the crocodile variety, signifying a hypocritical nature.

Now to examine the colour. 'Weak' coloured eyes in young persons are significant of weakness of character, which often shows itself in failure to 'play the game'. The person with weak coloured eyes is liable to 'go back' on friends and associates, if anything is to be gained by so doing. Do not forget, however, that all eyes weaken in colour with advancing years.

There is much truth in the saying 'true blue' in connection with eyes. Eyes that are really blue are almost invariably found in persons of a straightforward, steadfast and constant nature. There are two shades of blue in eyes—light and dark—and it is the dark blue which is 'true blue'. Really blue eyes are extremely rare, and many so-called blue eyes are merely blue-grey—that is, a blend between the pure grey and the rare pure blue.

Grey eyes can indicate a sad moodiness of disposition, selfishness or thriftiness, according to other signs. Grey eyes often accompany a dreamy, poetical nature, together with a want of practicability. Grey-eyed persons are more likely than brown-eyed to leave things unfinished, which had been started in a burst of enthusiasm. Nevertheless, grey eyes are associated in some persons with singleness of purpose.

Hazel eyes and talent go together; the cleverest people have hazel eyes as a rule.

All things considered, however, brown eyes are best. They are found in individuals with the most attractive personalities, with the most balanced characters. Brown hair was shown in the previous chapter to be the best from a character point of view. Dark brown hair and brown eyes go together. Grey eyes usually go with fair or light brown hair.

Brown eyes are indicative of a lovable disposition, a warmness of affection and a strong devotedness. To be the beloved of a brown-eyed person is to know true love which will endure.

Talent is particularly indicated by brown eyes which are flecked with green and orange.

The jet black eye, like jet black hair, is far rarer than is thought. When you do meet a person with eyes approaching blackness, beware! Not without cause have novelists come to associate black eyes with a black heart—in short, with villainy.

To turn now to the eyebrows; in considering these, we must pay attention to their curve, length, position, condition and whether they are separate or joined.

The gently curved eyebrow, if the hair is silky and the eyebrow narrow and finely marked, is

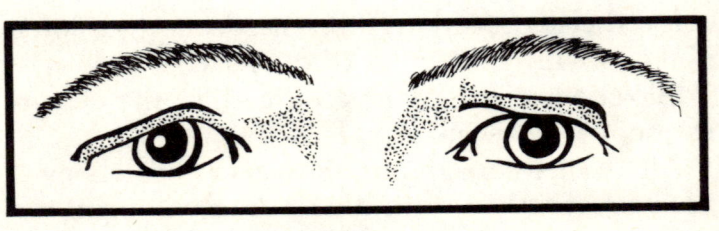

Fig. 13   Refined and artistic nature

indicative of an artistic temperament, one appreciative of beautiful things. Eyebrows which are curved, yet higher at their inner ends, are usually found in conjunction with other signs betokening a person of good taste, natural elegance and refinement. Fineness of eyebrow usually goes with fineness and delicacy of character. You never meet the bluff, hearty, coarse, but good natured person with delicate eyebrows.

The straight, thick brows which make a heavy line across the forehead are significant of an essentially practical nature. No dreamer this, but one who does things and gets things done; one on whom the word 'difficulty' acts as a spur and to whom 'impossible' is an unknown term.

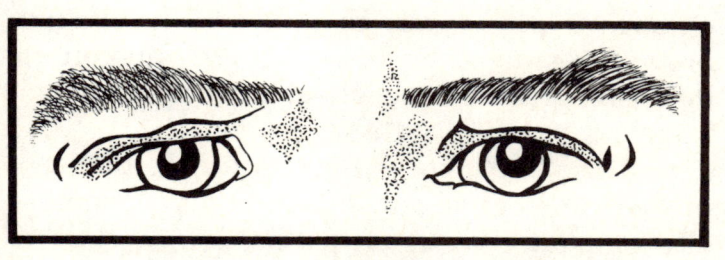

Fig. 14   Brows of an essentially practical person

As regards length, long brows indicate placidity of temperament, short brows hastiness. Long eyebrows, 'long' temper; short eyebrows, short temper.

'Open' eyebrows, that is, those quite separate and distinct from each other, are a sign of trustfulness, also of frankness. The 'open' eyebrowed person is open with you, and expects the same treatment in return.

'Closed' eyebrows which run together are characteristic of a suspicious nature, the reverse of trustful. This person is always searching for the ulterior motive, often when and where one does not exist. 'Closed' eyebrows indicate a covert nature, a want of frankness.

Powerfully marked eyebrows indicate strength of character, good or ill. Ill-defined brows signify general weakness—of vitality, of character, of will, and so on. Heavy brows mean power, intellectual and physical.

When heavy brows are also thick and shaggy, the more positive and dominating characteristics are indicated. Masterfulness, driving power and cleverness will usually be found in the shaggy-browed person—a powerful fighter when on the defensive and a person not at all likely to be 'put upon'.

Highly placed, curved eyebrows are one sign of weakness of will and a want of decisiveness—also of poor powers of observation, a want of

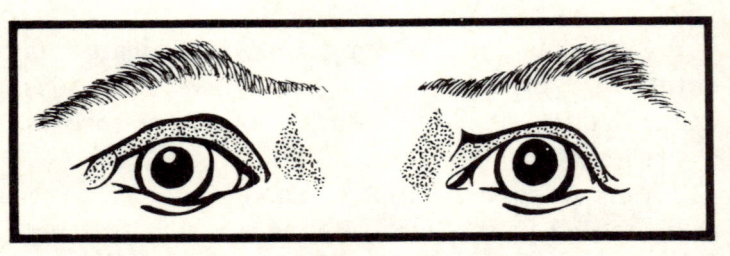

Fig. 15 Eyes and brows of an open, trusting person

penetrativeness. A person with highly-placed brows seems in a perpetual state of wonder and astonishment. That characteristic expression truly reflects their character—amiable blankness, rather than discernment and discrimination.

Thick, heavy brows which closely overhang the eyes signify excellent powers of observation. Little escapes these persons; they 'see through' things easily and possess the analytical faculty— the ability to take an idea to pieces. Two upright lines between low-placed brows, immediately above the nose, indicate strong powers of concentration. Notice how your brows tend to fall and to come together when you are thinking out a knotty point.

Short, thick brows are a warning of bad temper.

The low, straight brow, which is well marked without being bushy, is significant of firmness and determination. Such persons are not easily turned aside from their path; they may pursue it with a singleness of purpose which amounts to ruthlessness.

Brows which are neither high nor low in position indicate normality. Eyebrows which project (best observed in profile) are usually found on rapid thinkers, though some rapid thinkers have brows lying flat.

CHAPTER 5

THE NOSE AND EARS

NEXT to the eyes, the 'natural' character-reader pays closest attention to the nose. We have come to regard the big nose as a sign of strength of character, the small nose as one of weakness, the sharp nose as one of inquisitiveness, the pinched nose as one of meanness, and so on. As a matter of fact, these readings are accurate enough, in a general way.

First, let it be stated that the nose must be regarded in relation to the other features. It must be in proportion. When we speak of a small nose, we mean small for the face in which we find it. That same nose might be quite normal, or even large, in another face.

The types of noses are—Roman, Grecian, Retroussé, Syrian, Snub, Up-turned and Sharp. Just as we have combinations of the ruling types, so we have noses which are combinations of types.

The Roman nose is the eagle's-beak nose. The Duke of Wellington had a superb Roman nose. Generally speaking, the Roman nose is a sign of strong character, of aggressiveness. The quality

Fig. 16   Roman nose

of aggressiveness must not be confused with combativeness. There is such a thing as a 'mental fighter'—the man who fights hard against reverses, who does not knuckle down in the face of adversity but on whom setbacks act as a tonic, causing him mentally to brace his shoulders and hit back.

Where other signs indicate a person of predominantly mental or intellectual character, the Roman nose means a mentally aggressive person, an exposer of shams, a ridiculer of false conventions, an iconoclast. Where the signs, however, indicate one in whom things physical predominate, the Roman nose will signify physical aggressiveness. If the region of combativeness (in line with the ear, behind and about four centimetres from it) is strongly marked—well, 'beware of entering into a quarrel' with this person, for pugnacity and love of fighting are indicated.

The Roman nose is most often found in a successful person's face. Very colloquially put, 'the beak belongs to the boss'.

The Grecian nose is straight, and the easiest way to remember what it signifies is to associate it with the qualities for which the ancient Greeks (not the inhabitants of Greece of today) were noted.

The Greeks were great fighters, admittedly, but it was in the practice of the arts that they shone most radiantly. Greek drama, Greek architecture, Greek sculpture, Greek poetry, Greek oratory, Greek pottery—all are famous. The Grecian nose, therefore, is naturally accepted as signifying a leaning towards the arts, the more civilised, refined and coldly intellectual things of life.

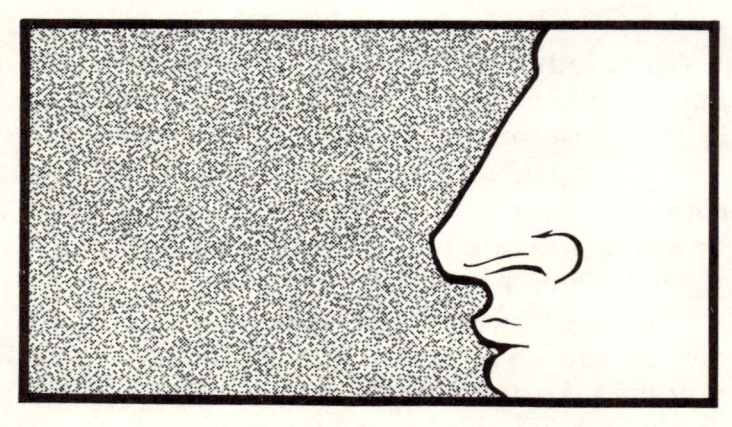

Fig. 17   Grecian nose

The Retroussé nose is the reverse of the Roman; it curves inwards. It is sometimes called the Emotional nose, because the emotions of the possessor are likely to dominate the intellect. This person is more likely to follow the dictates of the heart than the head. It is often found in persons of a cheeky and impudent character.

Fig. 18   Retroussé nose

Unless the inward curve is very pronounced, when weakness of character is indicated, the Retroussé nose often accompanies tenacity of purpose and some talent. The person with the Retroussé nose will usually succeed in getting his or her own way, but by the exercise of sly diplomacy and cajoling rather than by the aggressive methods which would come naturally to the Roman-nosed person. Persons with this kind of nose often have considerable charm of manner, which helps them materially to get their own way. This type mean to get their own way but prefer to get it without any unpleasantness.

The Syrian nose is the straight, drooping nose—seen in profile the tip is lower than the junction of nose and lip. This drooping nose belongs as a rule to the person with the drooping, i.e. melancholy, sad disposition. If the tip is pointed, an 'acid' sarcastic nature is indicated. The Syrian-nosed persons are mistrustful and suspicious. Their long nose signifies penetrativeness, but they will not come to a decision very rapidly on what they learn. Their natural cautiousness is all the time urging them to 'think it over' once again.

Fig. 19 Syrian nose

The combined Roman and Syrian nose is the real conqueror's nose, indicating one both ruthless and revengeful.

The Snub nose is a sort of neutral nose, from which we can learn little. When the Snub nose is small, with a sunken bridge, a very ordinary, commonplace character is indicated. If, on the other hand, the nose is of the 'bulbous' or heavy snub type, marked literary ability may be looked for. This nose indicates a certain want of delicacy and refinement, but it is by no means incompatible with talent. If there is a perceptible tilt to this nose, a sense of humour is indicated. The broad tip-tilted nose almost always goes with a vein of comicality.

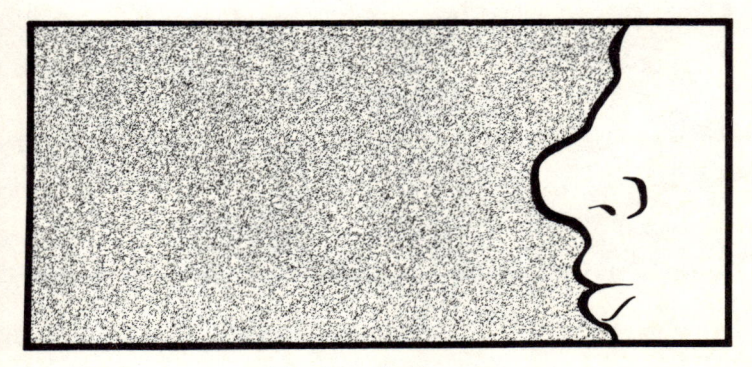

Fig. 20   Snub nose

The Up-turned nose (it all turns up, not merely the tip) is a sign of an optimistic, impressionable, enthusiastic nature, when it is fairly broad and full. The Up-turned nose should not be confused with the Retroussé nose, from which it differs in that it is straight and not curved.

The Sharp nose, narrow and with pinched nostrils, is the 'catty' person's characteristic nose. When it is tilted, revealing long, narrow nostrils, spitefulness is indicated. The long, sharp nose belongs to the 'nosey-parker', malicious, back-biting gossip. The broad nose is good, the narrow nose is bad. The masculine qualities of strength, courage, endurance, and so on, are usually absent from or heavily discounted in persons with narrow noses.

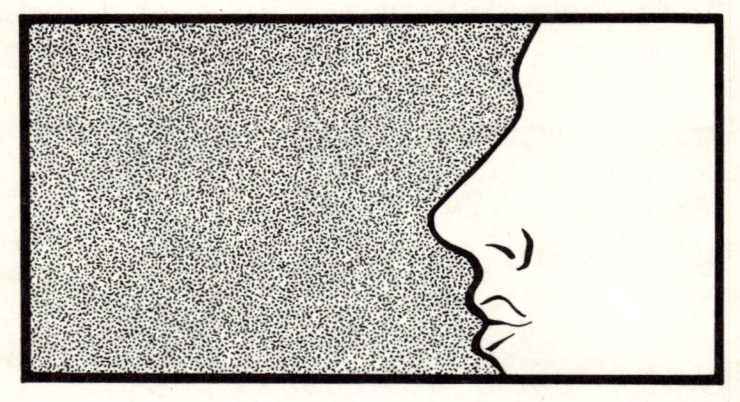

Fig. 21   Up-turned nose

Open nostrils, signifying good air-consuming powers, are indicative of vitality. Deep-chested persons with wide nostrils have an abundance of energy, and drive through to success. Narrow, pinched nostrils signify the reverse.

When wide nostrils are accompanied by a drooping septum, the analytical faculty is strongly indicated.

We can learn something from both the size and the position of the ears. Generally speaking, the 'quality' of the ears is in agreement with the quality of the character. Refinement and intellectuality is indicated by small, delicate, pale ears. Materialistic tendencies, amounting sometimes to coarseness, are signified by large, heavy, hairy, red ears. Small pale ears mean that the spiritual or intellectual part controls, large red ears that the 'flesh' is dominant.

Small ears are one sign of an affectionate disposition, and when the lobes are red (a sign of vitality, this), the affection will be of an ardent nature.

Disproportionately small ears are a sign of timidity. If the person with small ears also has a long neck and a small, straight nose, the timidity is confirmed.

Small ears are often found on persons of a thoughtful, reflective nature. Large-eared persons seldom have creative minds; they are the listeners, the 'takers-in', as opposed to the 'givers-out'. For the refinements and more subtle enjoyments of life they have little or no use.

Once more the middle course is best, and the average-sized ear, of a good pink colour, is best.

Ears stick out, lie close to the head, or are normal. The more the ears stick out, the more the possessor is likely to be self-centred. This indifference to the feelings and wishes of others can amount to positive cruelty when the ears are large and red, as well as sticking out. Normal ears, that stand clear of the head, upright, without sticking out, indicate possession of what may be termed the positive virtues—affection, courtesy, energy, ambition, honesty, and so on.

Close-lying ears, those that seem to be pressed flat against the head, should be looked for in order to confirm the qualities of diffidence, shyness, sentimentality and a reserved nature.

As regards position, ears that are set low down and well back are indicative of talent and brains. The greater the distance from the middle of the ear to (i) the top of the head, and (ii) the base of the nose, the greater the mental capacity. The ear placed high and forward is characteristic of the bad-tempered, callous, cruel person, particularly if the ears stick out. Observe both ears; one large and one small ear would indicate an unbalanced, unstable nature.

CHAPTER 6

THE MOUTH, LIPS AND CHIN

THE mouth and lips have the deepest interest for the student of physiognomy. Certainly the closest attention should be paid to these, for we can learn a great deal from them.

No great skill is required to read something of the character from the mouth. The prim, 'prunes and prisms' mouth of the precise person, or the leering, gaping mouth of the sensualist—who could mistake them?

Artists are very fond of 'cupid's bow' lips, and not improperly so, for the person with this mouth is invariably well-disposed and good-natured, if at times inclined to frivolity.

The mouth with upturned ends is found in persons of a happy, smiling and cheerful nature.

Fig. 22   Cupid's bow lips—good nature

The mouth with down-drooping ends indicates sadness and melancholy; a miserable, gloomy disposition. The dead straight mouth indicates, with full lips, firmness; with thin lips, hardness and cruelty. Remember that there is such a thing as mental cruelty.

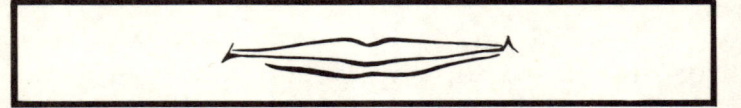

Fig. 23   Straight thin-lipped mouth—a hard nature

Do not look for or expect mental alacrity in persons whose mouths drop open readily. They are of the stupid, easily imposed upon type (unless, of course, there is a physical reason for it, such as enlarged tonsils or adenoids).

The person with the mouth habitually open, displaying large front teeth, is often a vainglorious individual and a boaster.

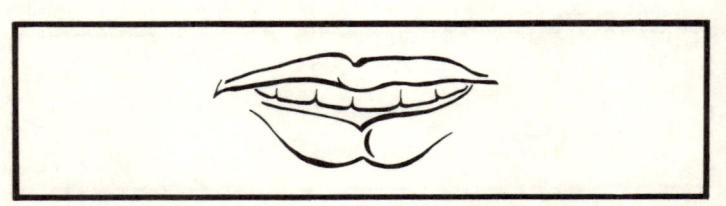

Fig. 24   Mouth of the gossip or tale-bearer

The 'ever-open' mouth is not good. The natural and correct conclusion to draw is that the person is 'open mouthed'—that is, a chatterer, a gossip and a poor confidant. Never tell secrets to the open-mouthed person, unless you want them broadcast. Persons of this type are better talkers than they are thinkers.

The tightly closed mouth is indicative of secretiveness and hardness. This type can hoard a scrap of information for years, until something is to be gained by disclosing it.

The normal mouth is lightly closed, and is best. Lips habitually closed indicate courage and decision.

Thick lips are a sign of sensuality and of passion. A disproportionately thick underlip is one sign of self-gratification in material things. Lips that are drawn in, making of the mouth a thin, straight line, betoken coldness, bitterness, harshness of temperament—a cruel, calculating, callous nature. Theirs is the studied and refined cruelty which hurts most—red-hot needle thrusts rather than bludgeon blows.

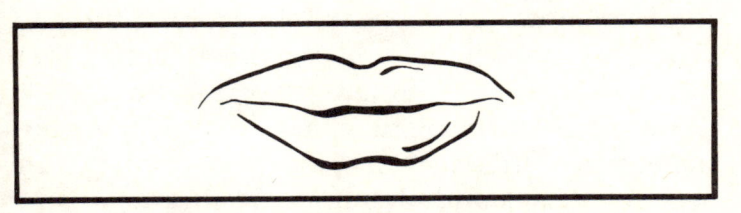

Fig. 25 Thick lips which signify sensuality

Full lips indicate a love of good things, a desire for an easy, comfortable existence and a strong measure of self-sufficiency. The heavy, full-lipped mouth not infrequently belongs to the egotistical type, who has a wonderful idea of his own acumen but who lives by appropriating the ideas and decisions of others and passing them off as his own. Lips that are brilliantly red and oily-looking indicate the glutton.

Where the top lip projects or overhangs, a pleasant, agreeable sort of temperament is indicated. Slight protrusion of the under-lip is not a bad sign, indicating some strength of will and determination, together with a balanced character, prudence and a strong sense of what is good for the possessor. The markedly projecting under-lip, however, reveals strength of mind carried to the length of mulishness.

One or two points about the teeth are worthy of attention. Regular teeth signify normality and the possession of methodical ways. Persons with perfectly even teeth are naturally systematic. Uneven teeth, very irregularly disposed, are usually a sign of uncertainty of temper. Protruding teeth are generally accepted as a sign of acquisitiveness, the capacity for acquiring things.

In this connection, you must remember that the teeth which are sometimes displayed are not those provided by nature. You may reasonably suspect beautifully even, perfectly shaped teeth of being false, and therefore decline to accept them as evidence of a good character.

Now let us examine the chin. It is a common error for persons to attempt to read character from the chin alone. Many a man has earned a reputation for strength of mind, when his jutting chin, accompanied as it was by a bulging brow, was merely a sign of stubbornness.

Refer back to the sketches of the three ruling types on pages 12, 16 and 19. In the Motive type, we have the square chin; in the Vital type, the round chin, and in the Mental type, the pointed chin. We can thus allocate to these three chins the dominant characteristics of the types they represent.

The man with the square chin we shall expect to be strong-willed, but with a powerful sense of duty, an admiration for what is straight and above board, a contempt for slyness and craft, and so on. When his squareness of chin is accompanied by top cranial development, we must expect to find him living a life of stern morality, and insisting upon all about him doing the same.

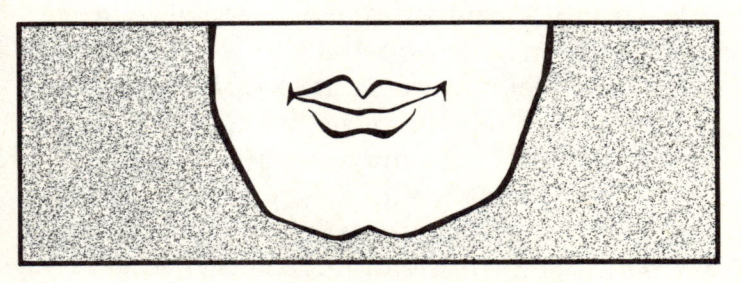

Fig. 26   Square chin of the Motive type

The 'old-fashioned', sternly religious, unbending father was of this square-jawed, high-crowned type.

The man with the round chin we shall expect to find predominantly Vital in type—fond of good living and creature comforts, with plenty of energy, bright, full of enthusiasm for what appeals to him, excellent company and hospitable. When his roundness of chin runs to a double chin, we may expect to find his love of good things carried to the point of self-indulgence. Where the bottom lip is pendulous, the heavy drinker is indicated in many instances.

Fig. 27 Round chin of the Vital type

It is quite wrong to regard a small chin as a sign of absence of will power, without having regard to other features, particularly the breadth and height of the forehead. Men of the predominantly Mental type have pointed chins, but in many instances it would be manifestly unfair to accuse them of being weak-willed. The fallacy has developed, in my opinion, because persons of the (practically) pure Mental type live very largely intellectually. By this I mean that they find all their interests in life in things mental and intellectual, as opposed to things physical and material. For this reason they are prone to regard things material as of little or no consequence and are therefore quite willing to be over-ridden on these points, because, to them, it is a matter of indifference which way it is. But oppose them intellectually, and you will find that there is a far different tale to be told.

Generally speaking, the square or squarish jaw betokens a leaning towards the solid, material things of life, while the pointed jaw is indicative of impracticability and idealism.

The small chin is one sign of timidity, and when accompanied by a long neck and small, pale ears, the timidity is confirmed. The small chin must not be confused, however, with the receding chin.

The small, round, protruding chin indicates a self-indulgent nature and a strong inclination to have one's own way. In women, this rounded chin has sometimes a rosy hue, similar to the cheeks, when a love of life and pleasure is indicated.

Fleshy chins are not good, being indicative of weak natures. It is the bone in the chin which determines strength of character.

The prominent chin, when accompanied by good cranial development, indicates the intellectual fighter. When the cranial development is not good, and the forehead is inclined to bulge, we have the physical fighter. The more pronounced the chin, the greater the capacity for 'seeking trouble'. We may be certain that the man who, coming upon several struggling men at a street corner, asked one of the combatants if it was a 'private' fight, or could 'anyone join in', was of the bulging-brow-and-jutting-chin type.

The normal chin is that which, without jutting out or receding, is full and firm. The unmistakably receding chin goes with a weak heart action, so that it signifies want of vitality, and weakness amounting to feebleness. The backsliding chin and the sharply receding forehead, when found together, indicate an extremely low order of intelligence.

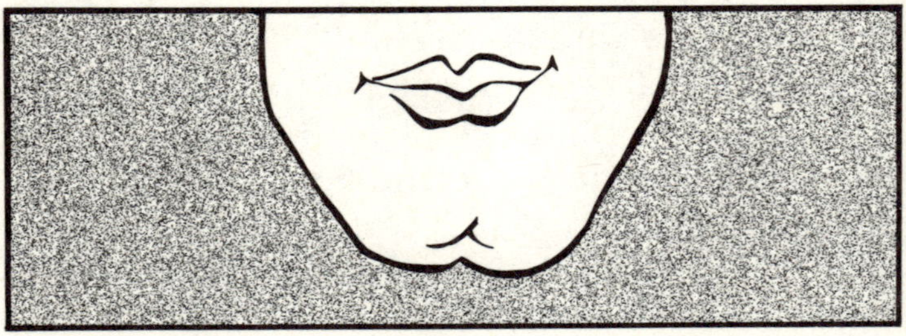

Fig. 28   Normal chin, slightly pointed

The full rounded chin is evidence of a genuine enjoyment of life, of energy and determination, and is an excellent confirmation of other positive virtues. When the man whose intellectual development indicates that he ought to succeed has a full, firm, rounded chin, you may safely say that he will succeed.

A pointed chin may indicate selfishness. The person predominantly Mental is frequently selfish, though it is only due to thoughtlessness. He is absorbed in himself, so wrapped up in his own thoughts that he does not realise that others are being neglected.

Persons with flat chins are usually undemonstrative and dry in their wit. They are both self-complacent and self-sufficient. They tend to independence of spirit.

When the chin clearly goes in under the lip and then comes out again, full and round, originality is indicated.

Fig. 29 Chin which indicates originality

To sound once more the warning note—do not attempt to read character from the chin alone.

CHAPTER 7

THE HANDS AND GESTURES

AN important part of character judgement concerns the hands. From the shape of the hands and fingers we can learn much, from their condition even more, and from the way in which they are used in speaking—for they are used in this connection—some final illuminating points. Staff managers and business executives who interview applicants for employment frequently pay the closest attention to the hands. There is such a thing as a capable hand and a cultured hand, and we should learn to recognise them.

Open-handedness or generosity is naturally signified by the hand which is habitually open when in repose—that is, when the owner of the hand is in a calm and tranquil state of mind.

The open hand is also indicative of honesty, especially when there is a tendency to keep the hands in view all the time. The business man who talks to you with his hands resting easily and naturally on the desk or table before him is usually to be trusted. At least, this sign can be used to confirm others, such as squareness of head and frame. The man of the predominantly

Motive type usually has his hands open and well in evidence.

The closed hand is one of the signs of a greedy, grasping, covetous nature. The miser has lean crooked fingers, ever curling to grasp real or imaginary gains. There is a physical reason for this, as for most signs—obviously the nerves and muscles have been starved.

The completely concealed hand is, generally speaking, a warning of a dishonest nature—not necessarily criminally dishonest, but perhaps morally and ethically dishonest. The hidden hand is suggestive of deceitful practices and 'underhanded' methods. But some men of fine character, but of a nervous temperament, partially conceal their hands—for example, in their coat pockets—in order to combat a tendency for the hands to fidget. In these cases, however, the thumb is usually left visible and we have not the completely hidden hand of the deceiver.

Bony hands which show marked ridges down the backs, especially when the fingers are long and nervous, usually belong to persons very insistent upon their own rights. They are precise in everything they do connected with money—the type which will have a 'settling up' to the last halfpenny. If two pence are due to them, they will have it or know the reason why.

Beware of the person who seems to be scratching at the table with curved fingers. There you have a covetous nature.

Hairy hands are a sign of vitality and strength.

White, hairless hands signify a poor supply of vital force. This, of course, does not apply to women, in whom white hands practically free from hair are natural and normal.

The clenched fist is invariably and correctly associated with anger, and the closed hand, when it is large and strong, is indicative of energy and force. Whether the closed hand means this or covetousness—as described above—must be determined by reference to characteristics displayed in other features. The natural fighter walks about with closed fists.

When considering the shape of the hand, one of the first things to which you should pay attention is the relative length of fingers and palm. For character reading purposes, when depending upon outward and visible signs, the length of the finger must be taken from the crease which appears when the hand is slightly closed to the extreme tips, and the length of the palm the other way—from the crease at the base of the fingers to the first crease of the wrist.

Measure your own hand and you will discover one of three things: (i) your fingers are longer than your palm, (ii) your palm is longer than your fingers, or (iii) your palm and fingers are of about the same length. Your two hands may differ in this respect.

Where the fingers are longer than the palm, we have a mind for details. Persons with this type of hand make excellent routine workers, for they revel in detail and are dependable and thorough. They are, however, unsuited to positions of authority, for shortness of palm goes with shortness of (mental) vision. They are prone to neglect the broader issues for comparatively unimportant details, which could and should have been delegated to subordinates. They are also given to hair-splitting on matters of no great moment.

The opposite type—the person with the long palm and comparatively short fingers—has the long and broad vision. Persons of this type are not good at detailed work, which they will quite openly neglect. But in positions of responsibility and trust, calling for initiative and imagination, they are excellent. Every long-palmed man should have a long-fingered person with or under him in order to attend to details.

A little practice in reading character will establish the habit of referring to the hands in order to confirm a conclusion provisionally drawn from some other feature or features. There is the big, broad, capable hand of the man who makes and does things with his hands; there is the pale, nicely-rounded hand of the artist; there is the large-palmed hand of the man born to control others, and so on.

Where the fingers and the palm are of about equal length, we have a balanced character—a certain breadth of vision, with some capacity for taking pains in small things, and so on. Nothing very remarkable or brilliant in any direction is to be expected of the man with the balanced hand.

Something can be learned from the shape of the finger tips. These can be rounded, square or 'spatulate'. The round and the square are easily recognised. The spatulate finger tip is rare, and is broader at the top of the nail than at the base. Very often the top joint is heavier altogether than the rest of the finger, with a pronounced filbert nail.

The round tip is indicative of things mental, emotional and artistic. Some absence of virility and driving power, however, is indicated, and the person with the pure round finger tip does not as a rule get very far for this reason. In some persons, the finger tips are pointed or conical, and these should be regarded as of the round type, but carried to the extreme. The more pointed the finger tip, the more unlikely is any measure of material success, because application to purpose and industriousness decrease as the finger becomes more pointed.

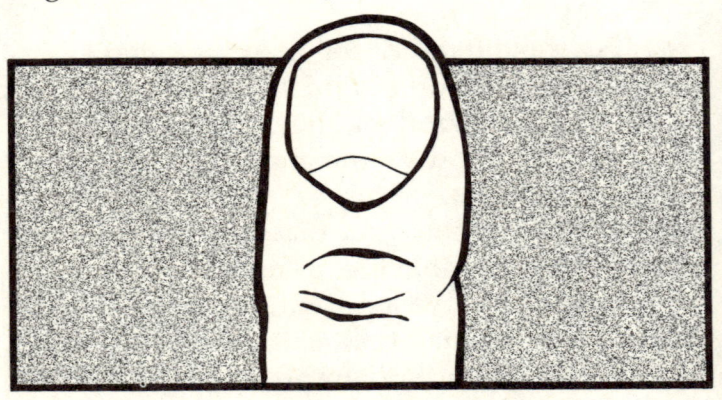

Fig. 30   Round—or Mental—finger tip

The square finger tip is good. It belongs to the person who is shrewd and has common sense. This person knows what is good for him, knows what he wants, goes out for it and gets it. Accuracy, firmness, preciseness in conduct and other positive virtues are indicated. The square-tipped finger is usually found on the man who has 'got on' and has consolidated his position.

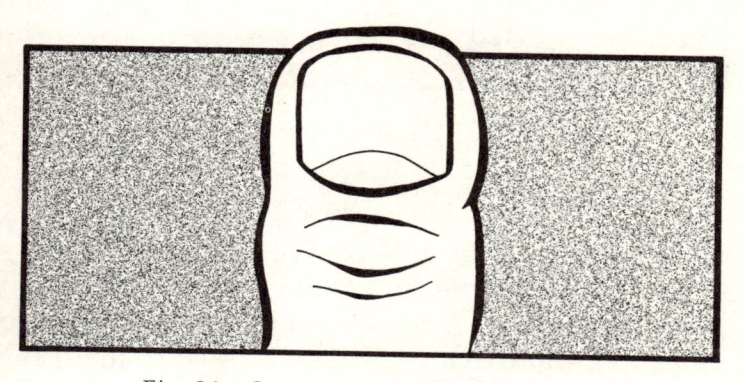

Fig. 31   Square—or practical—finger tip

The spatulate is the finger tip of cleverness. The person with this type of finger tip is the born leader, the born commander, the 'top dog' in whatever walk of life his inclinations may have led him. The spatulate finger-tipped individual is essentially material, far-sighted and intensely practical. Where the head that is high at the top-back is firmly set on the shoulders of a person with spatulate finger tips, you may safely say: 'Here is one who will drive to the front irresistibly.'

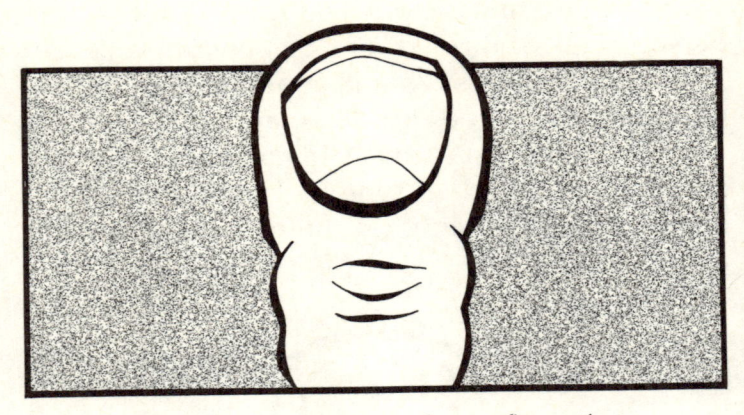

Fig. 32 Spatulate—or clever—finger tip

Thumbs, like fingers, reveal character. The long thumb and fine character go together. A big thumb is the sign of a strong man; a small insignificant thumb that of a weak individual. In a woman a big thumb is a sign of masculinity. Breadth in the middle joint of the thumb indicates firmness and will power. The thumb in which the middle joint is waisted—that is, the sides curve inwards—is one sign of mental obstinacy; it is useless to reason with such people, for there is an entire absence of mental elasticity.

The thumb that is 'loose' and moves very freely and independently of the rest of the hand is one sign of an independence of spirit, a bold and original thinker. The thumb which stands out at right angles, very low down on the palm, is a certain sign of adaptability.

Generosity amounting in some cases to extravagance is indicated by the thumb which curves backwards and outwards. Straight thumbs signify normality and freedom from excess in any form. The thick, short, heavy thumb may indicate cruelty. In this case, look for ears which are large, red and sticking out, with the combined Roman and Syrian nose.

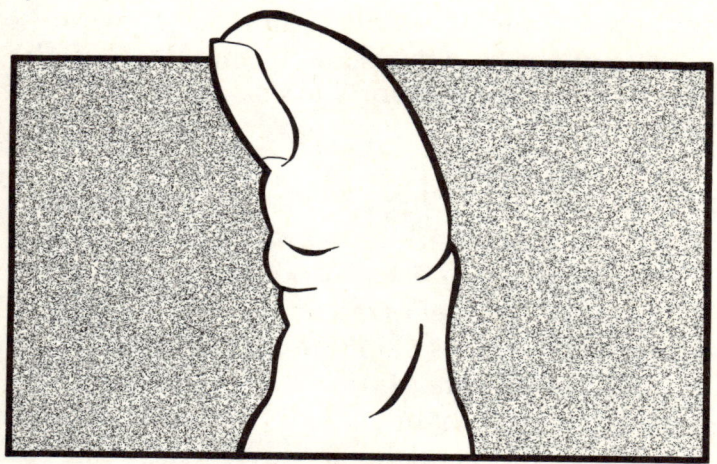

Fig. 33 Backward curve of thumb indicates generosity or extravagance, according to amount of curve

Much can be learned about a man's character from the way in which he shakes hands. There are many kinds of handshake—the flabby, hearty, the pump-handle, the 'linger-longer', the spasmodic, and so on—they all mean something.

The flabby, limp-fish hand extended to you to shake, but which does not shake yours in return, is generally indicative of a flabbiness of character, an absence of vitality and driving force. These people may achieve some measure of success when circumstances are all in their favour, but they do not shine when it come to a stern, uphill fight against odds. They are prone to forsake the substance for the shadow; they are lacking in grip.

The cold, lifeless hand signifies a poor physique, a want of vitality, and therefore of the energy which makes for success. Persons of the predominantly Vital type never have cold, lifeless hands.

The condescending 'I don't-do-this-sort-of-thing-as-a-rule' kind of handshake clearly betokens a person of a vain and pompous nature, full of pride and self-sufficiency. As this type of individual indicates vanity in a score of ways, we are quickly able to confirm the impression received from the handshake. The worst type of condescending handshake is that which extends fingers only. Beware of this person, for a mean, secretive nature is indicated.

The formal handshake, firm, but lacking real cordiality, of a mere moment's duration, indicates the man of reserved temperament, undemonstrative, but in all probability quite a fine character when it opens out. The tentatively extended hand betokens shyness and diffidence.

The hearty handshake is one quite easy to interpret. It indicates the hail-fellow-well-met type of person, but be quite certain that the heartiness is not a pose. There is also the man who shakes hands with you by drawing his hand back to somewhere in the region of his right shoulder, and plunging it down as though he is using a saw. Not a very deep or subtle person this, but one who does not doubt the pleasure it is giving you to meet him.

The pump-handle handshake belongs to the man who is over-demonstrative—a rather shallow and insincere individual. This sort of up and down handshake, without much grip in the fingers, is indicative of a colourless, unimaginative disposition.

The 'linger-longer' handshake is a peculiar one. This man shakes hands with you but does not let go of your hand, retaining it in his own. One of two things is indicated, and you must determine which it is by other signs and deductions. The individual may be of the 'leaner' type, lacking independence of spirit and initiative. His retention of your hand will be illustrative of his reliance upon you—he tries to retain your aid, as symbolised in your extended hand. Alternatively, the 'linger-longer' handshaker may be seeking to make use of you for his own ends. He tries to draw you to him, not because he feels the need of moral support but because he seeks to exploit you. Occasionally, among friends, the prolonged handshake is merely a sign of warm regard. It may also be found in a person of naturally affectionate disposition.

Lastly, there is the spasmodic handshake—in

several parts. Very akin to the 'linger-longer' handshake, this shake-pause-shake-pause-shake kind of grip indicates usually a person of unstable temperament—one who is likely to 'blow hot and blow cold'. It is also found as a sign of nervousness and a want of emotional control.

To come now to gestures: with some practice of character judgment, and the study of human nature which it essentially entails, facility in interpreting gestures will be automatically acquired, when the exponent will find that a person's gestures and hand-wavings provide helpful confirmation of suspected traits. The point I am about to make is that we should read character from gestures largely subconsciously, while devoting our conscious attention to the shape of the head, type of nose, and so on.

The person who illustrates his remarks with pointed and precise gestures reveals a precise nature. Extravagant gestures are in British people a sign of an extravagant nature and a certain want of control. Sometimes they reveal strong emotional feeling—such as whole-hearted enthusiasm for the subject being discussed. The orator not infrequently indulges in sweeping gestures when 'worked up' by his enthusiasm for his subject.

It will be realised that in reading character, full allowance must be made for natural and racial characteristics. The Italian, for example, gesticulates far more than the phlegmatic Englishman, and a person of a Latin race who does not gesticulate should be regarded with suspicion.

Restrained gestures, which are emphatic in their quiet way, are typical of the person who knows his own mind and who can display firmness without bluster.

The wild, flail-like gestures of the political or religious fanatic are easy to interpret. They indicate instability of character, or the possession of a certain amount of frenzied energy when the speaker is sincere. Whether he is sincere or not must be learned from other signs.

A marked absence of gesture may mean two quite different things—a sort of bovine nature which nothing can move to a display of emotion, or else perfect self-control. No difficulty should be experienced in distinguishing between the two. The phlegmatic or bovine person will usually have a flat sort of face when seen in profile, with rather heavy but pale features. The eyes are usually weak in colour and the eyebrows lightly marked and placed high. The expression is one of mild wonderment. The other kind of person, whose non-use of gestures is because of rigid self-control, will usually have a straight, hard mouth, with a firm chin and a somewhat prominent nose. The eyebrows will be well-marked and low down, over piercing eyes.

Don't study a man for character-revealing gestures when he is quite calm and tranquil. Get him excited over something, and then the true man will come out.

It is easy to understand how a highly strung,

nervous and excitable temperament will reveal itself in the gestures. Quick, purposeless movements and twitchings are typical. The frequent and quite unnecessary adjustment of the watch or the ash tray, the squaring of the blotting pad with the edge of the desk, the moving of the telephone a fraction this way or that—these are signs of a temperament predominantly nervous—that is, the brain and nerves are in the ascendent, not the muscular system.

Signs of the nervous temperament must not be confused with signs of an irritable and impatient nature—not infrequently found in persons of the predominantly Mental type. Irritability is displayed in conscious and ostentatious fidgeting with papers, tapping on the desk or counter with a pencil, drumming with the fingers, and so on. Nearly always, however, this type will display that irritability in their speech and general demeanour.

Nervous gestures that are obviously unconscious indicate a certain want of self-control but not of nervous energy. Such nervous persons are very frequently brilliant brain-workers, and the unconscious physical movements are, in reality, a useful form of exercise, keeping the muscles in good trim.

CHAPTER 8

POSTURE AND WALK

ONE of the best ways—if not the best way—of reading character is to obtain a number of general impressions of the person under examination and then to confirm or modify these by an examination of separate features.

In Chapter 2 we examined the three ruling types, and it had previously been explained that the object of making ourselves acquainted with the characteristics, physical and mental, of these ruling types was in order that we might read character from the whole as well as from the parts.

This attempt to begin our reading of character by classifying the subject broadly as Motive-Vital, Mental-Vital, or whatever we decided him to be, is one way of obtaining a stock of general impressions which we check off against our detailed reading from the features, etc.

Now we are going to examine two other sources of more or less general impressions—posture and walk.

The soldier-like, upright poise, habitually maintained, indicates a decisive character, self-control, a fine sense of dignity and self-respect, and an independence of spirit. When the head is thrown back slightly, we have dignity and self-respect emphasised, with maybe a touch of pride. Personal pride is not a bad trait at all; it is one of the essential ingredients of success.

Straightness of posture usually indicates straightness of dealing and a good moral character. This, however, must be confirmed. This type of man does not as a rule practise underhanded methods; he stands up to you and to reverses. If he is accustomed to stand with his feet more or less apart, strength of character and an independent spirit is indicated.

With women, however, this does not remain true. It is natural for a man to stand with his feet slightly apart, but a woman's natural stance, by reason of her somewhat different bony structure, is with her feet together. The woman whose habitual stance is with her legs apart may be suspected of a certain absence of modesty—it shows independence overdone, the defiance of convention.

The 'leaner' is not a good type. His favourite posture resembles a candle which has been standing in the sun. He keeps his hands in his pockets as a rule—one sign of a secretive, underhand nature. Whenever he is near a wall, he leans on it. He is seldom found engaged in business for himself without a partner; and he goes through life leaning on somebody else, often this person is his wife.

Some persons can remain quite calmly seated during a powerfully interesting conversation or discussion. Here we have either the phlegmatic type, which does not feel extremes of excitement or emotion, or the perfectly self-controlled type. These two types have already been discussed, and nothing need be added here.

Contrasted with the 'calm sitters', we have what I term the 'active standers'. The person of this type is usually predominantly Vital and so full of energy that it is continually seeking an outlet. Such persons remain seated for a few minutes at an important interview, but very soon they get excited or enthusiastic, and then they must stand up. They may even have to pace up and down, in order to let out some of the energy called up by their keen interest. This 'active standing' type of person is admirable in business; he or she does things and gets them done. Moreover, they convince others of their sincerity by their energetic enthusiasm.

The broad, deep-chested man is usually somewhat slow and heavy in his movements, but he is bold and courageous. The narrow, flat-chested man is nimble enough, but somewhat cautious and timid—a 'look-before-you-leap-and-then-don't-leap' sort of person. The slow, deep breather is the strong man; the rapid, shallow breather the weakling.

The man who cannot meet your glance when greeting you is either extraordinarily shy, or is not to be trusted. The self-respecting, honestly-intentioned man never hesitates to look you straight in the eye as he shakes hands with you. But don't forget that the bold rogue may also have this 'fearless' gaze; the rascal may deliberately act this honest-John, straight-eye characteristic. It is the man with the steady gaze, whether it is directed on you or not, who is to be trusted. The apologetic, self-effacing type is easily recognised, while detailed examination will usually reveal a weak, colourless character, a want of self-assertiveness, an absence of ambition and the will to succeed. The willing, conscientious plodder is of this self-effacing type.

The stooping, curved-back, studious type does not call for comment, nor does the blustering, bullying type. This last is easily recognised. He lacks finesse, and his domineering methods are patent to the man with any powers of observation at all.

We hear a lot today about the effeminate young man and the masculine young woman. From our point of view, that of character judgement, we need not take these very seriously. The effeminacy on the one side and the masculinity on the other is largely a pose. It is a sort of chrysalis stage as regards character. In short, the traits which older persons find so irritating will be grown out of and cast off when years of discretion are really reached. Few men of thirty can look back on themselves between the ages of, say, eighteen and twenty-two or three without saying—or at least thinking: 'What an insufferable young ass I must have seemed!'

At the same time, the man who carries slim-waisted effeminacy into his thirties should be given extra care in reading his character.

The snaky, boneless sort of person is not to be trusted, whether man or woman. When you see a person gazing about him with an open-eyed, open-faced expression, you may suspect a shallow sort of mind and no great depth of character. When you see a man walking along with his eyes on the ground, do not jump to the conclusion that he is a dishonest person who cannot look his fellow men in the face; a thoughtful disposition is indicated. The first individual gazes about for something to entertain and amuse him, for he has nothing much inside his head to give him mental occupation. The second individual, however, has a well-stocked mind, and can turn his thoughts inward with both pleasure and profit.

Nonetheless, there is a warning in an excessive disposition to keep the eyes fixed on the ground—a warning to the observant judge of character of a melancholy temperament, given to morbid introspection and of a fearful nature, dreading vague things.

The 'planner' and the 'opportunist' are temperamentally opposed. The former goes about his business with unhurried deliberation. He knows exactly what he is going to do, because he has thought it all out beforehand. The latter, however, lives for the moment. A quick thinker, with good forehead and bright alert eye, he pounces on the opportunity when it presents itself, and acts as it occurs to him to do on the spur of the moment. The quick, alert man, with the rapid, dancing gaze, is the opportunist.

It is quite easy to read something of a man's character from his walk. The slouching gait of the ne'er-do-well serves as an example. Contrasted with it we have the firm, purposeful striding of the man who has both self-respect and an aim in life.

The firm, heel-down, but quiet walker is a man of good character, determined but not aggressive, with ambitions but no desire to achieve them by riding rough-shod over other people. The stamping, flat-footed walker is often a bully and a blusterer. The man who wears down his heels very quickly is of the energetic type and in all probability he is predominantly Vital.

The man who takes long strides is usually very ambitious, but sometimes his judgment is at fault. He is too anxious to 'get somewhere' to pay all the attention he should to the direction in which he is going. Remember, however, that length of stride must be considered relative to height. What would be a long stride in a short man would be normal in a tall man. Similarly, a man's stride, height for height, should be longer than a woman's.

The rapid walker, who probably takes three steps to the long-strider's two, is also a rapid thinker and a man who knows what he wants.

The heavy, firm walker who makes plenty of

noise is a self-opiniated, self-regarding sort of person who has little thought or consideration for others.

The person who darts along with his head some way in advance of his trunk is of the pushful, thrusting type. Quite often his thrustfulness amounts to downright rudeness. His 'push' does not always mean success, for the simple reason that it is often ill-directed—or not directed at all.

Persons of the phlegmatic or predominantly Motive type are usually very deliberate and rather slow walkers. It is characteristic of them to take their time and to refuse to be hurried.

Then we have the ambler or dreamy walker. Suspect him of being predominantly Mental, and not at all Vital. He will usually turn out to be a wonderful schemer but sadly lacking in practicability.

The man who walks with very short, rapid steps is nearly always of the pompous and self-important type. If diminutive stature is also found, the egotism of the individual will be more pronounced. This does not apply to women, however.

The 'darter'—the person who dashes at every opening when walking on a crowded path without troubling to see if it is possible to get through—is the opportunist, the man who lives for the present, and who does not look far ahead or think much of the broader issues. He usually has the short palm and longer fingers of the person with a mind for detail.

Do not confuse the 'darter' with the energetic, active man who walks rapidly. He differs from the 'darter' in that he does not rush for each and every opening, but looks ahead and directs his course with care. He gets along faster than the 'darter', because he does not make futile dashes here and there.

The 'bull-at-a-gate' type of walker, who goes through you or over you as it were, does not call for detailed remark. His characteristic is physical force—not mental subtlety!

CHAPTER 9

THE CHOICE OF A PROFESSION OR PURSUIT

IF you have mastered the contents of the preceding chapters, you are well on the way to become a shrewd judge of character. What you now need to make you really proficient is plenty of practice.

While you are certain to obtain considerable interest and amusement from character reading—and the further you go and the greater measure of skill you acquire, the greater will be your pleasure—it has a very real utilitarian value. The ability to judge character is of the highest value to all who engage in business deals, particularly those which involve buying or selling.

For the salesman, the shop assistant, the buyer, the commercial traveller, the receptionist, the solicitor, the journalist, and for all in executive positions, the ability to read character gives a powerful advantage. It enables you to say that you *know*, and not that you merely suspect or imagine.

Then there is the extremely important aspect of self-analysis. You can learn to read your own character—in fact, you have been advised to make your first experiments in character reading with your own self as subject. By passing judgement on yourself, by recognising your weak points so that you may eliminate them or render them of no importance, by discovering your strong points so that you can take the fullest advantage of them, you can do much to ensure success in life. If character reading in this form of self-analysis was more commonly practised, there would be far fewer men and women in jobs for which they are unsuited temperamentally.

Do you suspect that you are a round peg in a square hole? Character analysis should help you considerably in choosing the right career, not only for yourself but for your children as well. Moreover, there is the vitally important factor of developing personal character; your most priceless possession is your individuality. You can discover your true personality, and become a real captain of your soul, by mastering the principles of character judgement detailed here. The important matter of choosing the right career will be returned to in a moment.

All our life, happily, is not spent in earning the wherewithal to live, and it is not proper that we should neglect to make reference to the social aspect. A great deal of what makes life worth living belongs to the social, as opposed to the business or professional side of our lives.

It is undeniably true that the man who is utterly devoid of the social graces is something less than a complete man. The man who is popular socially is almost always well-liked in business. Again, the man who is accustomed to move in good social circles invariably carries the charm and courtesy he learns there into his business dealings. Anything, therefore, which develops and expands the social side of our make-up will benefit us. Self-analysis, by revealing our weaknesses, and indicating how they may be overcome, does help us to develop personal charm.

There is, however, another aspect. To be popular, which means to be regarded as an agreeable and interesting person to know, one must learn to practise adaptability. It is a matter of suiting oneself to the company in which one finds oneself. Some few years back I came into contact with a man who was unquestionably most popular. I was not at all surprised, when I had an opportunity of a quiet talk with him, to learn that he was a very shrewd reader of character.

'It has become second nature with me, and I can't help it now,' he said. 'Immediately I am introduced to a man I begin to analyse him. Inside five minutes I have his character pretty well weighed up. After that it is a perfectly simple matter to get along well with him, because my reading of his character has told me exactly how to approach him in order to secure his interest.'

In considering the choice of a career, for oneself or one's children, attention may be most usefully given to the characteristics of the three ruling types, as detailed in Chapter 2.

As explained in that chapter, pure types are so rare as to be freakish today. But we generally find a predominant type in an individual, and it may be Motive, Vital or Mental.

Persons of the square—that is, predominantly Motive—type often succeed well in trade or business. They are also admirably suited to constructive work, such as engineering in its many branches. The square-built person, especially when the hands are large and the palms long, is the right individual to be put in charge of men. Persons of this type may lack the imaginative qualities essential to the origination and conception of schemes but they are thoroughly at home in bringing about the practical realisation of another person's theoretical plans.

Men and women of the predominantly Motive type are well placed in positions of trust, as managers, cashiers, and so on. For positions of responsibility in factories, this type is very well suited. They belong more to the productive side of industry and are not particularly good brain workers, though they are usually capable organisers.

The squarish person is not noted for social graces, and positions calling for charm, tact and diplomacy are not well filled by this type. The powers of self-expression are not usually very marked and few teachers are of this square type.

Persons of the Vital or round type are not so mechanically dependable as those just described, but they have other traits which give them superiority in certain directions over either of the other types.

It should be clearly understood that there are professions and pursuits particularly suited to each of the three types; it is solely a matter of finding the right calling for yourself, or your children, according to whether you are predominantly Motive, Vital or Mental.

The predominantly Vital type is, generally speaking, a very affable, charming and likeable person—cheerful, optimistic in outlook and usually an easy and pleasant individual with whom to get along. For this reason, the round-faced person is invariably a success as a commercial traveller, as a salesman, a sales manager, a special representative—in fact, in any position where charm of manner is likely to be an asset. Professional men, such as doctors and solicitors, gain by having a strong dash of the Vital temperament in their make-up, because it endears their clients to them.

Persons of the predominantly Vital type should not be in positions where method and routine are all important. This type, by reason of its vitality, is impatient of restraint and finds monotonous employment absolute torture. They are diligent and energetic workers when well suited but are hopelessly ill-suited in a routine job. They should be engaged on work which takes them out and about and brings them into contact with other persons.

The predominantly Mental type provides us

with our brain workers. It does not follow that every person in whom the mental part predominates has a brilliant brain. Quite often we have mediocrity in the predominantly Mental type, and then the brain work will be of the ordinary, everyday, clerical variety. 'Office work' is the natural vocation for men and women of this non-brilliant mental type.

Mental power of a high order, indicated by considerable forehead development, wide and high, fits the possessor for the highest positions. Great thinkers of all kinds, brilliant scientists, physicians, lawyers, inventors, writers—in all these the mental part predominates.

To sum up, if you are predominantly Motive, get a job where you can take charge of those who are doing things. You are cut out for the higher realms of manual work, for constructive effort.

If you are predominantly Vital, your greatest asset is your power to charm and so to persuade. Get a job in which your success will be measured by your ability to get other persons to behave as you desire.

If you are predominately Mental, use your brains. Seek employment where thinking is far more important than doing. Consider the professions of analytical chemistry, medical research, journalism, the law, and so on.

Our effort to help you can best be rounded off by repeating a word or two of caution. In character reading, get your general impression first, but always confirm it by an examination of individual features. Never attempt to judge character from one or two signs only. Study them all, and let your judgment be the sum total of your reading and interpretation of them all.

INDEX

acquisitive 60
adaptable 72
affectionate 25, 34, 37, 44, 55, 75
agreeable 60
aggressive 31, 46, 48–9, 50, 64, 68, 82, 84, 85
ambitious 30, 84
artistic 27, 45, 50, 70

bad tempered 34, 47, 56, 60
benevolent 24, 30
boastful 58
build 13, 15, 19
business, success in 14, 17, 81

candid 39
cautious 52
changeable 17, 32, 34, 35
character reading, benefits 6–10
charming 51
cheerful 16, 17, 57
chins 26, 61–5, 77
comfort, love of 17, 62
comical 51, 53
complacent 65
conceited 25, 36
constant 32, 34, 43, 44
constructive 14
contemptuous 18
courageous 20, 31, 55, 59, 81
courteous 37
covetous 67, 68
cranial development 24, 36, 40, 61, 63

cruel 56, 58, 59, 73
cunning 28, 40, 41

deceitful 25, 40, 42, 67
decisive 59
deep thinking 20, 29, 32
delicate 45
dependable 68
dependent 75, 80
determined 64, 84
diffident 31, 74
dogged 13
domineering 34, 36, 46, 82
dreamy 35, 43, 85

ears 54–6, 63, 73
emotional 18, 33, 51, 70
endurance 31, 33
energetic 13, 16, 17, 32, 33, 36, 38, 55, 62, 64, 68, 81, 84, 86
entertaining 17
enthusiastic 17, 53, 62, 76, 81
eyebrows 14, 44–7, 77
eyelashes 42
eyelids 42
eyes 39–44, 77
  colour of 39, 43, 44
  descriptions of 16, 19, 39, 40, 41
  position of 39, 40
  size of 39, 40
extravagant 76

face 12, 15, 18–19, 77
features 12, 16, 19, 77

feet, small 16
fingers 71–3
firm 14, 71, 72, 77, 84
foreheads 25, 26–9, 30, 40, 62, 63, 64
frank 45, 66
frivolous 40

gaze 39–41, 82
generous 34, 37, 66, 73
gentle 33, 34
gestures 76–8
glutton 60
good company 17, 62
gossip 59
graceful 16, 19

hair 31–8, 39, 40, 43, 44
hairless 32
hands 16, 66–69, 86
handshake 73–6
hard 33, 59
hasty 45
heads 12, 16, 19, 24–6, 25, 26, 30, 71
hearty 74–5
home-loving 37
hybrid types 11–12, 21–3

idealistic 20, 25, 63
imaginative 20, 25, 27, 33, 35, 69
impatient 18, 20, 21, 78
impractical 34, 43, 63, 85
impulsive 17
independent 65, 72, 80
indolent 38
initiative 33, 69
inquisitive 48, 54
insincere 75
integrity 15
intelligent 13, 18, 20, 26, 30, 35, 43, 54–5, 56, 63, 71

intolerant 21
irritable 34, 78

jealous 38

lips and mouths 57–60
listless 35
logical 20

material success 13, 71
materialistic 24, 30, 55, 59, 63
mean 48, 67, 73, 74
memory, good 29
mental ability, lack of 25
mental superiority 18–19, 20, 21, 26
Mental type 11, 18–21, 22, 23, 61, 62, 65, 78, 85, 90, 91
methodical 60
moral 24, 61, 80
Motive type 11, 12–15, 21, 22, 23, 28, 61, 67, 85, 90, 91
mouth and lips 57–60, 77

necks 15, 31, 63
nervous 67, 76, 78
noses 48–54, 77
  Grecian 48, 50
  Retroussé 48, 51
  Roman 58, 50, 73
  Sharp 48, 53–4
  Snub 48, 52–3
  Syrian 48, 52, 73
  Up-turned 48, 53

observation, powers of 14, 28, 42, 47
obstinate 24, 26, 72
open air, lovers of 17, 32

opportunist 83–4, 85
opposite sex, attraction to 19
organiser 13
original 66

passionate 34, 38, 59
peace, lover of 33
penetrative 52
perceptive 29, 35
personal magnetism 16
phlegmatic 77, 81, 85
placid 45
planner 13, 83
pleasure-seeking 17, 35, 40, 63
ponderous 28
posture 80–4
practical 13, 14, 45, 69, 71
precise 67, 69, 76
profession, choice of 87–93

quick-thinking 20

racial characteristics 34–5, 76–7
refined 20, 45, 54–5
reflective 29
religious 24
responsive 37
romantic 27, 37
ruling types 11–21, 22, 23, 79
ruthless 52

sad 34, 38, 43, 52, 58, 83
sarcastic 52
scientific 29
secretive 39, 59, 73, 80
selfish 25, 43, 65
self-assertive 36
self-centred 37, 55, 60
self-controlled 77, 80, 81
self-effacing 30, 82
self-indulgent 62, 63

self-opinionated 14, 45, 73, 85
self-reliant 14, 33
sensuous 42, 59
shallow 83
shy 31, 55, 56, 63, 74, 81
slow thinker 28
spiritual 24
spiteful 53
sporting 17
stolid 14, 28
straightforward 43
strong 31, 32, 34, 37, 46, 48–9, 60, 67, 72, 80
stubborn 26, 28, 60
studious 27, 40, 82
stupid 40, 58, 64
suspicious 46, 52
sympathetic 33, 37, 42

talented 44
teeth 60
tenacious 37
thoughtful 55, 83
thrifty 43
thumbs 72–3
trusting 42, 45
trustworthy 66

unstable 56, 76, 77

vain 74
villainous 44
virile 33
Vital type 11, 15–18, 21, 22, 23, 36, 61, 62, 74, 81, 84, 85, 90, 91
vitality 15–16, 17, 18, 54, 67
   lack of 30, 41, 46, 64, 68, 74

walk 84–6
weak character 43, 46, 48, 51, 63, 72, 81, 82